AF417729

# A WEEK TO A MILLION DOLLARS

*Reprogram your mind for wealth and success*

"it's not just a book... it's medicine."

**ONYANGO OWOR**

# A Week To A Million Dollars

## *Reprogram your mind for wealth and success*


Copyright ©2021 by Onyango Owor.
www.onyangoowor.com
onyango@onyangoowor.com
+256 787 367 458

ISBN: Softcover;  978-9913-623-08-7

  HardCover  978- 9913-623-09-4

  eBook  978-9913-9978-0-5

All rights reserved. No part of this book may be used, reproduced or transmitted in any form or by any means, electronic, mechanical, magnetic or photographic, including photocopying, recording or by any information storage and retrieval system, without prior written permission from the copyright owner.

The scanning, uploading and distribution of this book via the internet or any means without the permission of the copyright owner is illegal and punishable by law. Please purchase only authorized electronic editions and do not participate in or encourage electronic piracy of copyrighted materials. Your support of the author's rights is sincerely appreciated.




*"it's not just a book… it's medicine."*

# CONTENTS

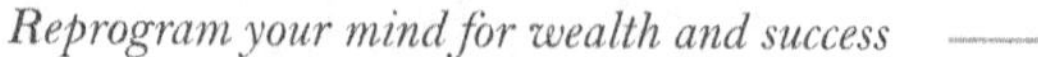



*"it's not just a book… it's medicine."*

# DEDICATION

This book is dedicated to all those who are ambitious and hardworking yet feel stuck-unable to progress or achieve financial freedom. Be inspired!

# PREFACE

I will never forget that week: The week that changed my life. Up until that time, I had not made much progress in life – in my career, financially, spiritually and socially. Even though I had been working for a while, there was nothing stimulating, exciting or interesting in life. It was the same straight line that was boringly predictable. It seemed as if I was stuck in a maze: fighting so hard but never able to break free. Although I was making some money, it was as if the money was just passing in between my fingers and then disappearing where I knew not. It felt more like running on a treadmill – lots of sweat but no actual distance covered. Days turned into weeks, weeks into months and months into years. The frustration kept building. Whereas some of my friends seemed to be making progress, I felt like the years were just passing me by without much measurable progress. What is wrong with me? Am I stuck in the rat race? I wondered.

Weaving through traffic, I finally slowed down behind a Ford truck as my thoughts became present and conscious. Since I was not in a rush, there was no need to overtake the truck. The road trip was soothing on this bright and sunny Tuesday afternoon. The clouds seemed to be putting up a performance for me, showing me the different shapes that



*"it's not just a book… it's medicine."*

they could come up with when I got closer to them. I loved getting out of town. The wind out there is different. The natural vegetation is therapeutic. I had gotten accustomed to hitting the road to my country home every fortnight or so just to refreshen my mind. Could this be what financial freedom means? I thought to myself.

Several years have passed since then and now I am my own boss working just because I love to work, but not because I have to. When I work, it's to flourish and create impact but not to survive. Now I have my own law firm and run several businesses, real estate investments being one of them.

But how did it all begin? How did I launch my journey to wealth and success? How was I able to start with almost nothing and reach where I am today? What is the one thing to which I can attribute all my success? How did I start "without capital?"

I was first exposed to the idea of habits when I was a little boy of about 3 or 4 years. As it is in many cultures, mealtime is when every family comes together. I always anticipated that this would be both an appropriate and exciting time for my siblings and I to talk about the adventures of the day and brag about our triumphs over to each other in the presence of every family member. Unfortunately, we were never allowed.

"Jelani!" I alerted my little brother, ready to declare my victory of the day over to him.

"Shut up!" Mother would immediately interrupt. "Those are bad eating habits," she added. "Never talk while eating", was her favorite meal-time word of caution.

So, I grew up knowing that one of the bad eating habits is talking during meals. If there are bad habits, then there must be good habits as well. My child-like mind had wondered. After hearing these words of caution for so long, I felt I needed more clarity. One night after dinner, I asked, "Mom, what are habits?"

She frowned. As was her manner when we asked her a serious question, she sat me down on a small stool in the kitchen and went ahead to give me a lecture that seemed to last for eternity. I don't remember a single word she said.

The next time I searched about the word "habit" was when I had become an adult. You see, I had been in the habit of setting countless goals but attaining none. I would write new year's resolutions in January only to cancel them before the end of March. "This year doesn't look good for me, let me wait for next year," I told myself. "Next year is my year," I added. This went on for many years I cannot count.

In a bid to achieve my numerous goals I even extended my year to a fourteen month's calendar. For example, my calendar year ran from January to February the following year. By this, I supposed that life would be somewhat better than what it was only to end up disappointed. I felt trapped and lost. How long is this going to last? Till retirement? I anguished within me. I wasn't willing to wait any longer. How about the monthly bills? How about the unfulfilled dreams I had? How about the successful and happy life I promised myself to live? How was I ever going to achieve all these? Why was I ambitious and hardworking but still unsuccessful? All these and many more were the questions that ran through my mind.

One day, I got into a financial crisis and needed to borrow some money to solve a pressing and immediate issue. I looked around for someone who could lend me the money I needed – just $2,000 – but I could not find any among my friends or colleagues. Habitually, I had recklessly lent out money to dozens of people from all walks of life. Now I needed some and none of them could bail me out. This was partly because, like me, they were working but did not have any savings. Others had savings but I wasn't a reason good enough for them to withdraw the money. 'Birds of a feather flock together', so goes the saying.

After running around without succeeding, I turned to a client of mine. Having worked with him for several years I well knew his financial position. He was wealthy and had a grip on the money game. During our numerous professional engagements, I had noticed how happy he and everyone else at his company were. I wanted to be like him. Secretly, I admired him. Like him, I too wanted to run my own successful businesses. I had always wanted to ask him how he has been able to accumulate so much wealth in such a short time, but I had never gotten the chance to. I was timid and afraid of what my wealthy client would think about me in inquiring about his wealth.

Knowing how rich he was, I was sure he would lend me the money. "$2,000 is like a drop in the ocean to him. It won't be a problem." I said to myself. However, it wasn't an easy thing to bring myself to that moment of humility—to ask for a hand up from my client. Was it even ethical? Well, when you are in dire straits, such questions take a different degree of priority in life. My mind seemed to have located the source of my respite and I was determined to swallow my pride and explore this unpopular option of asking my client for money.

This book is an account of how my client ended up guiding me from where I was then, to where I am now, starting with nothing but a desire to change my life for the better. It is an account of the observations I made about him and other wealthy clients with whom I have interacted in my practice and during the course of my other business ventures.

Everyone wants to be successful, wealthy and rich, but few people have discovered what it takes to build that empire. Successful people have mastered the art of reaching the top in their professions. Whereas many have done it in totally unrelated fields, others have done it simultaneously. It is not an uncommon thing to find a businessman who has become successful in four or more enterprises. It is not an uncommon thing for a top salesman in one company to cross over to another company and still top the charts. It



*"it's not just a book… it's medicine."*

is not uncommon to find those politicians who never lose elections - who seem to have mastered the art of winning the hearts and minds of the voters. It is not uncommon to find that Artist who releases hit-song after hit-song. But why do these individuals seem to get it right every time?

People say that there are no shortcuts to success, that you have to take the long road. Well, it depends on your definition of success. Let us take an example: If you knew for sure that you would never fail at anything and that whatever you start would get accomplished, which of these two options would you choose: Becoming financially free in thirty years or becoming financially free in five years? Many, if not all would say, "Of course five years!" The reason society highly rewards innovation is because it is human nature to want to attain our goals within the shortest time possible, and that means we are constantly looking for a more effective way of accomplishing tasks.

This book is about habits – habits that when incorporated into your daily life – will hasten your journey to financial freedom. It is arranged chronologically to get you from point A to point B in your financial journey. As you read, think of how you will start implementing the habits immediately. Keep an open mind, and you can join the company of the rich in record time.

xii

# ABOUT THIS BOOK

I wrote this book because people from all walks of life have asked me the same questions. Some of these are: How did you become rich? Why is my life stuck in the same position? How can I escape mediocrity and start excelling in my field? I earn a lot of money but can't tell where it goes. How can I get out of debt? How can I become my own boss? How do I experience growth? How can I exhaust my full potential? How can I start a successful business with little or no capital? Is it possible to attain financial freedom?

If you are reading this book, chances are high that you have asked yourself or know someone who has asked these very questions.

I have been saddled by debt, felt desperate and confused because I knew I had not fully maximized my potential. I have felt lost for not knowing how to attain financial freedom. However, through a journey of self-discovery and education, listening to and observing my wealthy client, I placed myself on the right path to financial freedom.

This book is written in simple language; you will not find references to complex theories or metaphysics. It is a book for all. After all, the truth is straightforward and so are the rules and principles of wealth acquisition. There is no magic or mystery about the attainment of wealth yet so many people remain stuck in poverty; unable to afford even the basic necessities of life. Many are even afraid of attempting to find out how to improve their situations. For the bold and brave, let this be the start of your lifelong journey to success and financial freedom.

The structure of this book is inspired by Buddha's method of problem-solving which involves four steps;

1.  A realization that there is a problem. Some people don't even know that they are living a life of limit, are trapped in a rat race or in financial slavery.

2.  An understanding of the cause of the problem. Whereas some causes may be real, others are artificial. Understanding the cause of the problem first and fast is important because it will lead us to search for a permanent cure.

3.  Visualization of the end result when the problem is solved. When we finally picture what our lives will look like when the problem has been solved and, believe that it is possible, then we shall have travelled half the journey. This is the genuine discovery of the unlimited potential we have. It feels much like the first flight of a caged bird.

4.  Practicing a certain procedure or method to systematically solve the cause of the problem to achieve the desired result. This is action. We must

 | *"it's not just a book... it's medicine."*

be willing to take the necessary actions in the right manner so as to obtain the results we desire to achieve. In this case financial freedom and success.

To get the most out of this book keep an open mind, be willing to learn, unlearn and relearn, question and practice independent investigation of whatever you read in this book, be true and honest to yourself, reflect and take immediate action where you need to change from some negative habit(s). The cumulative result for you will be growth, progress and finally financial freedom. Can you learn about these habits that can make you a millionaire within a week? Yes. All wealth begins with actioned imagination resulting from accurate and organized knowledge.

 *"it's not just a book… it's medicine."*

# MAN KNOW THYSELF

*"You must take personal responsibility. You cannot change the circumstance, the seasons, or the wind, but YOU CAN CHANGE YOURSELF. That is something you have charge of." – Jim Rohn.*

*"Nothing is predestined. The obstacles of your past can become the gateways that lead to new beginnings." – Ralph Blum.*

## Monday

By 7:22 am, I was already at the reception of his office. Being his lawyer, I did not need an appointment to see him. His secretary mentioned that he was still in a meeting, but I would be able to see him in a few minutes. After waiting a little while, his secretary came to the waiting area and ushered me in. I had made several trips to his office, but it still struck me with its uniqueness each time I entered it. The room was large and spacious. It had something exotic about it probably because most of the furniture and fittings were imported from France and the Middle East. Two of the walls were opaque, and the other two were made of glass, revealing an exquisite view of the city.

He welcomed me in with a smile, shook my hand and offered me a seat. We exchanged pleasantries and chatted a bit as he made me a cup of coffee.

"So, what can I do for you today?" he asked. Mr. Client had a habit of going straight to the point and sticking to business. No matter how close you were to him, he wouldn't give you more than a few words of greetings.

I had been reciting the pitch throughout the night, but suddenly I wasn't so confident anymore. I was feeling kind of uneasy. My hands trembled slightly. In a short while, I would know my fate and I dreaded the fact that a "no" was one of the options for my request. It's never a comfortable place to be when you are totally out of control of your life and fully depending on someone else's mercy and grace to bail you out. For a man, it is embarrassing, even emasculating of sorts. It is simply humbling.

"Mr. Client, I need to borrow some money," I started with a shaky voice.

He leaned forward, placing both his hands on the large office desk. "Tell me about it." He urged me on with a brief smile

 *"it's not just a book… it's medicine."*

as if he had anticipated that this day would come. The ball was back in my court. I had expected this uncomfortable exchange to last less than a minute. I would present my request and he would let me know my fate in an instance. However, here I was with a herculean task to justify my ask before Mr. Client. Uncomfortable is not a word succinct to describe what I was feeling. I am sure embarrassment was written over my face and I discovered that thinking on my feet would be the savior of me in this instance. I had to gain his trust that I would be a good debtor.

"I am in a bad financial situation and I need a bailout." I continued. I went on to explain to him why I needed the money and the plan I had designed to pay him back. I even offered to work for him for free on the next assignment estimating that $2,000 would be the worth of this next assignment.

"I really need the money. I am in a bad financial situation." I added. I was feeling really desperate.

"I understand." Mr. Client commented. "But first, how did you get here?" he asked.

"Get here?" I inquired seeking more clarity.

"Yes." He responded after taking a sip of coffee from his cup. "How did you end up in this bad financial position?"

Those words hit me hard in the mind. I reflected on my entire life in an instant. It was thus far filled with reckless expenditure and a lack of a definite purpose and goals. I froze for another second or so, unable to respond to one of the simplest questions I have ever been asked. I had passed my law exams with little effort and won my first court cases without breaking a sweat. Why was this simple question so hard to answer?

How did you end up here?

This phrase which is familiar to most of us might have been worded slightly differently here but has the same meaning. Many people have struggled financially, many are currently struggling, and many more will find themselves in a similar position sooner or later. It is not because they want to - far from it - everyone wants to be successful. Human beings are naturally creatures of growth and success. From goals such as weight loss, getting promoted, overcoming a bad habit or writing a book, to big goals such as starting a business, buying out your competition, climbing a mountain, buying a private jet, traveling the world or becoming the richest person on earth, everyone wants to succeed at what they are doing. But why are most people not achieving the successes they desire? Why are most people not ticking off their goals?

Many folks want to be wealthy, but they don't know their current financial stand. Many want to lose weight, but they don't know how much they weigh currently. Still, others want to get out of debt, but they don't know how much money they owe. Many people want to get married, but they don't even know their current relationship status. Many have adapted the phrase "It is complicated" to refer to something that even they themselves don't understand.



*"it's not just a book… it's medicine."*

If you are reading this book, chances are you are not contented with something or some area in your life. But before we start to make changes, we must first recognize what exactly it is that we want to change. Now is the time to take a complete inventory of your life. Ask yourself this question: Am I happy and contented with my life in the areas of finances, career, family, spiritual and ethical, social and cultural, physical and health, mental and educational? Mr. Client's voice woke me up from my brief reverie.

"How did a brilliant lawyer like you end up in such a situation?" He asked again. "I have paid all legal fees on time." He added. Mr. Client was the only client in the whole of my career who always paid more than we charged him. However much we charged him, he always paid more. His wealth seemed to increase despite countrywide outcries of an economic downturn. He seemed to earn much more money than he could ever spend. I felt rather ashamed of myself first for being broke and secondly, for not having an answer to Mr. Client's simple question. I knew that he was not being condescending to me but there was a genuine care in his countenance. For a minute, it seemed as if he wanted to know exactly what the root cause of my financial problem was. This is not what I expected. Men at times "understand" each other's shame and embarrassment and for the most part, cut their conversations short to save the day. They tend not to be vulnerable to each other. My situation was lingering over the two of us like an open book. However, instead of feeling like the ground should open up and swallow me, I had this warm feeling like I was in the presence of someone who cared. I had anticipated the transaction to last two minutes or so, but it seemed as if it would take even longer. Silently, I was resolving in my spirit that I would never have to be in this situation again, but I felt like Mr. Client was mature enough to accommodate me.

You are the captain of your ship

I placed my cup which was now empty on the table and sat back leaning in the soft chair. Then silently repeated the question to myself, how did I end up in this financial crisis?

"The economy is bad. This country is no good." I responded after a long pause, thinking I had it all figured out. But even as I spoke those words, I knew that there was no conviction and belief in them. I just wanted to answer the question and get the discomfort in our rather icy conversation out of the way.

Mr. Client smiled and said, "But how come I am not complaining about the economy? How come countless people have made it in this same country that you are saying is 'no good'?" Can you not see the countless commercial and residential buildings springing out of every part of the city? He asked

I quickly realized I had been making excuses and they were the very ones hindering my progress.

So, if the country is not the problem, why am I not successful? I questioned myself.



*"it's not just a book… it's medicine."*

Several answers came to my mind. Could it be my teachers' fault? Was it the way I was raised? Was I stuck with the 'wrong' boss? Maybe where I come from is the problem. Or is it the system? I probably could have chosen the wrong profession. Is it my colleagues at work? Or I didn't have the right clients. I was trying to come up with a logical explanation as to how I had ended up in this bad financial situation, but I could not find one that made sense even to me. All the reasons I found seemed valid, but were they true?

Five minutes must have passed. Mr. Client realized that I had hit a snag and wasn't going to give him an answer any time soon. To save me from a mental short blockage, he cleared his voice as he got up from his chair and walked to the whiteboard on the wall to my left. He picked up a red marker and wrote in bold letters the word **'RESPONSIBILITY.'**

I read the word out aloud, "Responsibility!" and asked, "what has it got to do with my current situation and request for a loan?"

"Most people never take responsibility for their lives and as a result, live unsuccessful and unfulfilled lives." He responded. "Where there is success or failure, you will always find the root cause of it from the point of responsibility. Those who are successful take responsibility for attaining it but those who are not, do not take responsibility for their failures thus far. Most people want success without an ounce of responsibility in it." He added.

I sat up and became more attentive, knowing that Mr. Client was simply being polite by referring to "most people." "Most people" was actually me. I was part of the wretched of the earth—owning no means of production, influenced but not influencing, led but not leading, consuming but not producing anything of value to the world, controlled but unable to effectively control myself.

"Unfortunately, many argue that they are in control but in reality, they have let go of the controls and are just floating through life. I am yet to meet a successful person who is not taking full responsibility for his or her own life." He continued.

He was striking a raw nerve somewhere.

Then he drew a rough sketch on the board of a ship in the sea and said, "Think of a ship in the sea. It requires a captain, a compass and a sail to reach its desired destination. Imagine a ship with no captain, compass or sails; that ship will not reach its desired destination. The winds will blow it here and there, it will move fast with fast winds and slowly with slow winds until it ends up in an unwanted destination. Many people are like this ship. Interestingly still, some people are like a captain in a ship with no compass or sails, and yet they claim to be in charge of their lives. So many people just float through life, being driven here and there by the day-to-day's economic or behavioral winds. By accepting whatever life throws at them, they end up floating in a direction that they did not want in the first place. And then after months or even years of being

   *"it's not just a book… it's medicine."*

blown in such a manner, they suddenly end up in unwanted destinations." He concluded.

"Like a bad financial situation," I responded. His point was beginning to make sense to me.

"Exactly." Said Mr. Client nodding in approval with a brief smile playing on his lips. "It's never too late to turn your ship around. Remember, it is one ship and you are its only captain." He added.

This blew my mind. All along I thought I was in control of my life. I thought I was taking responsibility yet silently; I was blaming everything and everyone else except myself. I thought about all the times things have not gone my way. Was it because someone else wronged me, or because I had failed to meet the expectations? Was I cheated or I simply didn't come out as the best? Everything was suddenly becoming very clear.

"You probably have a solid reason why your life has turned out this way; Why you haven't been scoring your goals, or why you haven't yet become successful. I have been there before and back then; I was no different." He resumed. "I had my own share of excuses to justify my failure to attain my goals and become the kind of person I had always wanted to be. This was working against me because every time you make an excuse, you give up the power needed to change the direction of your life, the power needed to become the person you want, the power to achieve the things you want. In fact, 85% of the kids I grew up with earn less than

$30,000 a year. The majority are unhappy and unsatisfied with the choices they made and the opportunities they didn't pursue. We all seem to be 'responsible' for our lives, and yet when our lives are examined, it turns out that most of us are VIP members at the excuse club." I smiled sheepishly knowing exactly what it meant. I belonged to that club. Mr. Client continued. "As long as you continue finding excuses for why things haven't happened the way you expected them to, you will remain stuck. So, if you want to get out of any bad situation that you have found yourself in, begin by owning up to your results. Realize that your actions – or sometimes inactions – are the sole cause of your results. Then immediately cancel your membership at the excuse club. That's why I asked you the question in the first place. It is to help you reflect and know whether you are taking full responsibility for the results in your life or not." He concluded.

Mr. Client had many articles, quotes, pictures and printouts pinned on the wall inside his office. He walked me to the wall on my left and stood next to a poem by William Ernest Henley titled Invictus. He made me read it out aloud:

*Out of the night that covers me,*

*Black as the pit from pole to pole,*

*I thank whatever gods may be,*

*For my unconquerable soul.*

*In the fell clutch of circumstance*

*I have not cried aloud.*

*Under the budgeonings of chance*

*My head is bloody but not bowed.*

*Beyond this place of wrath and tears*

*Looms but the Horror of the shade,*

*And yet the menace of the years*

*Finds and shall find me unafraid.*

*It matters not how strait the gate,*

*How charged punishments the scroll,*

*I am the master of my fate,*

*I am the captain of my soul.*

He was right. For years, I had blamed government policies, the size of the economy, a rigid world economic order and lack of capital for being the reasons for my mediocre life. This blame game was so unconscious as if I had inherited it from somewhere. I saw how easy I had been critical of others and never used the same mean yardstick to review my own life and my input into it. I had to change my whole paradigm. The responsibility for my life's results was mine and mine alone.

What exactly do you want?

Today's meeting was quite different. I had gone to him asking for help. I needed help. What I thought would be a simple dipping in the pocket and writing a check was something that was turned on its face—Mr. Client dipped into my psyche using one question and unearthed the root of my trouble. Previously, I would be the one asking questions but this time it was Mr. Client asking the questions relating to my financial case. He was such a great examiner that one was compelled to reflect and discover their purpose in life and then set goals.

We were interrupted by a knock on the door. It was his secretary, Alice. She walked in like she owned the place. I knew from her employee file that she was in her forties, but she moved with the excitement of a teenager. She seemed to dance along as she walked. You could clearly see that she enjoys her work and it seems like she has been doing this all her life. Alice was always happy and had an unexplainable positive energy about her. I had never heard her complain about anything. She always went out of her way to ensure that all visitors to the office were comfortable and relaxed. Her positive attitude endeared her to her supervisor, Mr. Client, and won her his trust. He always trusted her with sensitive assignments and yes, she earned more than her colleagues.

"Sorry for the interruption," she started with an apology. Mr. Client smiled.

"Your meeting with Apollo from the Insurance company is in five minutes." She announced.

"Alright, thank you, Alice." He replied as she shut the door behind her.

 *"it's not just a book… it's medicine."*

"So, what exactly do you want?" Mr. Client asked me. "I can either give you the $2,000 you asked for or teach you everything I know about how to become financially free in record time. But not both. Choose only one." He added.

I immediately got mixed feelings. This is something I have wanted for a very long time. I have always wanted to learn what it takes to become successful and live a happy and fulfilled life, how to start and run big businesses, and how to make it to the top of my profession. I wanted to be wealthy, and now the very keys were before me. I wanted to be financially free. But I also needed the $2,000... I felt my heart sink. It is what I had come for. I was now torn between two options.

"Why not both?" I asked.

"Because my friend," he replied, that is what life is. Many times, you will be faced with two options: Enjoy now and suffer later or suffer now and enjoy later. Most people choose to enjoy now — which is short-lived — as opposed to enjoying later for the rest of their lives. Which is it going to be for you?" he asked.

Realizing that I had reached a point of no decision, Mr. Client smiled, then asked, "Why don't you go think about it, then we can meet tomorrow morning and you give me your response?"

I thought for a moment. At least I would get time to think about it. Then I responded, "Okay. Fair enough." I was feeling both happy and disappointed at the same time.

We agreed to meet the following morning at his office by 7:30 am.

I said bye to Alice as I walked past her desk, then out of the office.

As the day unfolded, Mr. Client's words kept ringing in my mind. "What exactly do you want?" He had asked.

His words reminded me of one of the laws of the universe: The law of attraction. This law is a philosophy that states that positive thoughts bring positive experiences or results whereas negative thoughts bring negative experiences or results. It goes on to state that people and their thoughts are made from "pure energy" and a process of like energy attracting like energy exists through which a person can improve his health, wealth and even personal relationships. There is no empirical science supporting the law of attraction, but Mr. Client believes in it. It is as if the state of your mind and your thoughts dictate the results of your life—consciously and unconsciously as well. Those who have absolute clarity about what they want will certainly have it. The issue is not about if they will get it, it is about when. Mr. Client had a great sense of clarity about what he wanted in life and he was not apologetic about it. It was not some general statements such as "I want to be happy". There were quantifiable and tangible things that he wanted. So, what exactly did I want anyway?

I remembered back then when I was a child when sometimes we would talk about someone and somehow the person

 *"it's not just a book… it's medicine."*

magically appears. This might have probably happened to you more than once. Or you might be thinking about someone and the person actually calls you on your mobile phone or sends you a text message. It has happened so many times that society has even coined a phrase for it. Whenever it happens, people say, "Talk about the devil and there he appears." Now that I know, I believe that it is the law of attraction in action.

So, if your reality is determined by your thoughts, what should you be thinking about? Many of us spend sleepless nights worrying about our debts, bills, responsibilities, obligations, the weight we need to lose, the bad habit we need to drop, where we fall short or the relationship has gone bad etc. What this actually does is compel you into a behavior that keeps that situation recurring.

For example, if you are always worrying about losing weight, chances are your subconscious mind - which is more powerful than your conscious mind - will automatically program you into doing the very things which will keep you overweight. This happens because what you dwell your thoughts on is losing weight, which means you have to be overweight in the first place. You can't lose weight which you don't have.

This is also true for the other areas of your life as well. If you are always worried about paying off your debts, your subconscious mind will program you into constantly getting into debt. Even if you are paying them off, you will always be tempted to get into more debt simply because your subconscious mind – where habits are formed – is aligned towards paying debts.

Napoleon Hill in his great book, *'Think and Grow Rich'* wrote, *'Truly, thoughts are things,'* and again, *'Powerful things that, when mixed with definiteness of purpose, persistence, and a burning desire for their translation into riches, materializes in the physical.'*

When I understood this, I again asked myself, what do I really want? To accept the $2,000 and solve my immediate problem, or to learn the steps necessary to become financially free and never lack for the rest of my life? Of the two options, I chose Financial Freedom.

As my head hit the pillow that night, I had a feeling a country boy has when he knows that he will be visiting the big city for the first time in his life. I had excitement all over me as well as eagerness. I couldn't wait to know exactly how I can become financially free. My teacher was ready and experienced. It showed that he was wealthy and he was not making any excuses about it. He was proud of it and yet so humble a man to 'stoop low' and give me such a great audience. I reflected that it must have taken him quite a bit of time to get to where he was. It was a mystery to me and that mystery is what I wanted to unravel. Whatever price there was to pay for me to get to Financial Freedom, I made a mental note that I would be willing to pay. The die was cast. I couldn't wait for the following morning.

   

I picked up a book beside my bed and tried to get a chapter done but my thoughts were unsettled. I just couldn't bring myself to concentrate no matter how much I tried. I found myself staring at the ceiling and dreaming of how it might be when I finally get financially free. I don't remember the time that I finally dossed off.

## Practical Steps to Your Million Dollars

1. Take responsibility of your life. The buck stops with you. You are in charge. Take full control of your life. Choose a date that you will get started on this journey and make it official. You are the CEO of your life.

2. Eliminate excuses from your life. Do not justify your shortcomings and failure. Own your life decisions. Write down all the blames you have meted out on people: your parents, your education (or lack of it), your spouse, your family, the government, your place of birth and origin, the dollar rate and so on. Look them over and declare that they are NOT responsible for your destiny. You are.

3. Replace all excuses with action. Let your life be action-packed towards the direction of your dreams. Make a decision to start aligning your actions with positive change.

4.  Get absolutely clear about what you want out of this life before moving forward with it. Decide what you want in this life. Don't move until you do.

5.  Choose to pay the price of what it takes to get what you want. Know what it takes to get to where you desire to go and pay the full price to get there.



*"it's not just a book… it's medicine."*

**CHAPTER**

# STARTING WITH A WHY

*"The two most important days in your life are the day you are born and the day you find out why."* – **Mark Twain**

*"To ask the right question is already half the solution of a problem."* – **Carl Jung**

## Tuesday

Arriving at Mr. Client's office the following morning, I had a determination that could only be surpassed by the curiosity that I felt about what it would take to be financially free. Dressed in a dark-blue suit, a white shirt and a matching blue tie, I was already feeling different and confident. I was optimistic. This was a much better psychological state that I was in as compared to the previous day when I was asking for money. Something exciting was about to happen in my life. This was the day that the Lord had made. And I was definitely rejoicing in it. I felt I was on the brink of something big. I was going to receive the keys to financial freedom but the responsibility to find and open the doors was mine alone.

I glanced at the wall clock. Time check: 6:10 am. I greeted Alice with a smile and sat in the waiting area, eager for my first lesson. I had always admired the whole office set-up, but there was something about it today that made it look different. Everything fitted in its position like it was part of the design for the building. Neat. Nothing out of place.

The office was spacious and well-lit and covered an entire floor. There were no partitions, except for the C.E.O's office and a glass boardroom. The secretary's desk was on the left… Right next to it was the waiting area. A transparent glass boardroom was opposite the waiting area. Several desks and cubicles were aligned in a street like formation – in rows and columns forming a joyful matrix. The office looked like a tiny city inside a building. Everyone had his or her own working space and everything was visible to everyone. It was incredible. I wondered what it felt like to own an office like this.

As I sat waiting, I remembered how I had spent most of the night awake wondering what to do. A tiny inner voice kept telling me to take the $2,000 which I needed urgently, but I kept reasoning it out and silencing it. I remembered

 *"it's not just a book… it's medicine."*

an article which I had accidentally come across. It was a piece by Gary Ryan Blair talking about EXCELLENCE. In it, he asked a pretty tough question; "If you are not committed to a life of EXCELLENCE, then what on earth are you committed to? Mediocrity? Average? Doing as little as possible?" He continued to say, "While the system or environment you find yourself in might push you to become mediocre, to settle for a lower standard…the best option is to always choose excellence."

"Success begins as a decision – one where you look at your life, business, and relationships and decide that everything you touch is going to be better, that the example you set is going to be inspiring, that the performance bar is going to be raised higher, and that the legacy you leave will be memorable and significant." He wrote.

I jumped to my feet as soon as I saw Mr. client come out from the boardroom. We walked together – exchanging pleasantries - to his office at the corner on the southern side of the building. Inside his office, he made me a cup of coffee and sat leaning back on his chair as if giving me the chance to speak first.

"I have made up my mind," I started, "I am ready to learn how to be wealthy and successful. It is something I have always wanted to ask you about but never got to it. Now that the opportunity has come, I want to learn how to be rich."

A big smile appeared on his face. It was as if one of his children had just returned home with an excellent report card at the end of the school term. He immediately got up from his chair and came to sit on the visitors' couch with me.

"Are you sure?" he asked looking into my eyes.

"I am absolutely sure," I replied in a firm and determined voice.

"Congratulations!" he exclaimed. "Welcome to financial freedom." He said holding my hand.

I did not know what to say except, "Thank you."

Then he asked me a rather simple but hard-hitting question,

"But first, why do you want to be successful?"

## Why Do You Want to Be Successful?

I had been asking myself this question the previous evening, and for a better part of my life and I had not yet gotten a satisfactory answer. To me, attempting to work towards financial freedom was postponing my current happiness for a dream that seemed too far for me – at least for now. I would probably wait for and work on it sometime in the future when circumstances are better. Why should I choose to postpone my happiness? I wondered. But wait! What happiness? I wasn't happy at all, I was miserable. I was barely surviving, I was behind on attaining my goals and fulfilling my obligations, and that is why I was trying

   *"it's not just a book… it's medicine."*

to borrow money in the first place. How about never having to borrow again in my life? Never feeling desperate again. I would love that. I would work hard for that.

Over the years, I have discovered that people choose to be successful for various reasons. A great percentage sought financial freedom because it would obviously solve their personal problems, much like the $2,000 problem I had. The truth of the matter is that many people have different degrees of financial problems. The only difference is the figures. People, therefore, look for financial freedom in order to alleviate this pressure out of their lives. The interesting thing about a large percentage of these folks is that they want this financial freedom through an event, and not a process. That's why they will look for a "Mr. Client" of their own to bail them out. Invariably, some do get the breakthrough through that event, but it is only a temporary reprieve.

Some people will resort in get rich quick schemes. Their hearts are entirely pure and sincere when they do this because they want to solve their problems sooner or faster. That's why betting and gambling is a big-time industry. A large percentage of the people who are betting their business capital away are those who want to solve a certain problem in their lives. Unfortunately, their approach is totally wrong in that it creates a vicious cycle. They wanted to solve a problem, but they end up creating the same problem. Not knowing what solution to use, they double down on the same mistake and gamble some more. In the end, the addiction that ensues is so huge that it ends up destroying them. They sincerely set out to be financially free, but they end up in a worse state than they started.

All these thoughts were rushing through my mind as Mr. Client waited for his answer. Up until that time, I had always wanted to rush in giving him answers to his questions on my personal life but from the previous day, I had learnt to be patient and answer correctly. I was also perfectly Ok with not having an answer for him. I wasn't in an examination room and he wasn't going to award me marks anyway. I was in a learning process. Probably, I wanted to have financial freedom in order to solve my problems. I thought that would be the case.

Whether in finances, social, political, health or relationships, many people view success as a pathway to getting rid of problems. 90% of our problems are financial, making many other so-called problems and issues secondary. Success is a requirement for most people because they want to bid farewell to their day-to-day problems. If you want to solve most of your social issues, solve your financial issues first.

Zig Ziglar said it best, "Money is not the most important thing in life, but it ranks up there with oxygen." I think Zig must be right.

I also quickly thought about another group of people who have a different reason for seeking financial freedom. They want to balance the scale. This simply means that they want to go for success to compensate for their past experiences.

 

Much as we hate failure, it is unavoidable. Failure is a large part of our daily lives. Success to these individuals is a way to soothe past failures. They kind of make an inner vow that they would not go through the pain that they went through as they were growing up.

Many people who grew up in less advantaged families have adapted the phrase "humble background" to refer to the poor families from where they come. To these individuals, success is a way of wiping away the years of strife, struggle and lack. They want to succeed in order to "give their families the life they never had."

They may have lost in the past, but in the end, they want to win. Success can compensate for all the previous failures. This is something that I strongly resonated with.

However, was balancing the scale such a strong reason for me to be a successful person? I honestly felt like even though it was a valid reason, I wasn't resonating with it much. I mean, if people want to be successful in order to balance the scale, that's their right and it shouldn't be taken away from them. I however thought and felt that if I lived up to that standard, it would be a lofty goal well enough for me to be motivated to attain it. In my heart, I felt like 'balancing the scale' just bordered around being 'better' than what I used to be previously. That was a less lofty goal for me and it was not the desire that I had in my heart.

Looking at the great things that Mr. Client was doing with his clout, it wouldn't make sense for him to mentor me only so that I can balance my life and compensate for what I did not get previously in life.

My mind quickly produced another thought. People want to be successful in order to live like the rich. Many people look at the lifestyles of the rich and they marvel, dream, desire and wish that it was theirs. In fact, there are various TV shows and Series specifically produced towards this end. We are shown how a rich man owns a yacht, a private jet, a posh house, vast business interests and so on. In our minds, these people have it made and there is no trouble in their lives. Honestly, who wouldn't want that kind of life? I most certainly was interested in becoming successful so that I can have the lifestyle of the rich and famous.

Many do not know how to achieve this though and therefore end up purchasing counterfeited items, expensive clothing and electronics. They think that the lifestyle of the rich is about showing off riches. You have probably seen how those who want to be rich pretend. Some engage in flimsy lifestyle wars trying to out-compete each other. They do what a personal financial guru Dave Ramsey famously said: We buy things we don't need to with money we don't have to impress people we don't like."

As I thought through this, I was not naïve to realize that I wanted the lifestyle of the rich. However, that was not going to be the reason for desiring to be successful, at least, it was not going to be the main reason for my seeking of success. There had to be something greater than that. I wasn't just about to start engaging in a virtual lifestyle competition for riches. There was no point to prove to anyone and even if there was, at the end of the day there was no use, no purpose, and no pay for it. Yes, I wanted to the lifestyle of the rich but that was not the main reason for seeking success.

I shifted slightly in my chair as Mr. Client observed me as if aware of the thoughts that were going through my mind. Certainly, he had interacted with many people the way he was interacting with me today and he had heard a wide range of answers to his question. In fact, he was so well versed with my situation because he was exactly where I was that Tuesday. It seemed to me like he had enough time for me and that he wasn't particularly in any hurry. It also seemed to me like this question, although seemingly asked in passing was an important question for which he needed an answer. For the first time in my life, I was actively considering an answer to this question. Previously, I had just done it in passing as if the answer was either obvious or that it was not important. Probably that was one of the reasons why I was in the situation that I was in at the moment. There was no strong "Why" in my life for seeking success and probably that's why there was no "X-Factor" if you will, in my work life. I did what I did in life as I walked through the motions of it—work, get paid, pay bills and repeat. Had I seriously considered why I wanted to be successful? I smiled as I realized that the world, I lived in had already given me a why since I was not conscious enough to find it myself. That "why" is the famous S-word, 'Survival'. I didn't have a compelling reason for seeking success other than to survive. In fact, the previous reasons I was deliberating on, the reasons as to why people sought success, are deeply rooted in survival.

I didn't want to be under the tutelage of Mr. Client as a mere financial survivor. I also thought about another reason why people want to be successful and even before the thought would fully develop in my spirit, I knew that I wasn't interested in that reason either. People want to be successful because they love the taste of winning. Again, there is nothing wrong with that for others, but for me, there had to be something larger than that. People want bragging rights – so it is called in sports. Human beings will do whatever it takes them just to be victorious. It is natural: victories pump our egos. And the biggest feeling comes from the recognition of our wins by our peers, subordinates, superiors, family and friends.

Organizations have mastered this. This is why companies have awards such as employee of the month, salesman of the year and so on. When an individual achieves success in any endeavor, the win itself may not be as important as the recognition that comes because of the win.

But here is the most sinister thing about such wins—they are moving targets. They are mirages. In other words, there is no end to this pursuit. It is like you are 'treadmilling' all your life. When you attain a particular goal, you look

 *"it's not just a book… it's medicine."*

up from your toil only to realize that either the goal posts have shifted or there is someone else who is effortlessly doing much, much better than you are. It is a life of vanity in the end but when you are deeply engaged in it, you do not notice how deluded you might be. I thought it would be very flimsy to just be successful so that you can have bragging rights! I wondered what standard could even be used to gauge that so-called victory. I wondered who would set those standards.

There was something about being in the presence of Mr. Client that just made me feel like I was having elevated thoughts that day towards my own life. It was amazing how one simple, but profound question had triggered a great introspection in my life that would unearth my reason for wanting to be successful.

After thinking long and hard, I found the simplest, and yet the most truthful reason I wanted to be successful. Looking into his eyes, I finally replied, "I want to be successful so as to achieve financial freedom."

Patting me on the shoulder, he slowly replied, "And you will. I know you will." I half expected him to challenge my answer, but he didn't. It seemed to me like there was no right or wrong answer—that the why had to be personal. Probably that is why he never commented on the answer I gave him, whether it was right or wrong, and probably that's why he never suggested or gave any clues. The why had to come from myself and I was glad it was that way.

As he assured me that I would attain my goal, there was a sincerity in his voice that I had never heard before. It made me feel at peace and confident. I felt strong. Immediately I got the feeling that I can never fail again in my life. I was in the right hands. I knew for sure that I was going to be successful, and Mr. Client was going to guide me. Someone believed in me. It felt good. This was a heaven and earth difference between trying to go on this journey alone. Leadership guru John C. Maxwell says that a leader is a person who "knows the way, goes the way and shows the way". Mr. Client was my leader in personal financial freedom quest for he had already gone the way and now he was showing me the way. What a blessing this was. To think that I had to debate within myself whether to take this mentorship or to take the two thousand dollars was simply preposterous, looking back. What I was receiving was far much more than I could have bargained for, and seemingly this was for free! I even started wondering what was in it for Mr. Client in doing this. He was a busy man with very many projects, interests and engagements. Why would he hive off his quality and valuable time for me? Suddenly, I felt like Mr. Client had just engaged the instructor mode in him as he launched the session building up on the answer that I had just given him.

He said, "Every great success begins with a decision to take responsibility for your life, followed by a strong WHY."

As I nodded in agreement, I quickly thought about most of the major decisions I had made in my life and how different



*"it's not just a book… it's medicine."*

the outcome would have been if only I had found a strong reason behind those decisions.

"What I am going to teach you is not a get-rich-quick-plan, but if followed and practiced consistently, over time, can quicken and ease your journey to financial freedom. Of course, there will be challenging times, that is just how life is. Just don't quit, instead, treat every experience as a learning opportunity and get back on focusing on your goals. Remember learning never stops." He added.

This was a massive boost for me. But it was also a radical shift in paradigms. The responsibility was mine. He could teach me, but it was up to me to make things happen. This built up my belief in myself. If he could do it, I knew I could do it too.

As soon as he was satisfied that I was in agreement, he got up, walked to the whiteboard, erased the word RESPONSIBILITY which he had written the previous day, and wrote these three letters: **W.H.Y.**

I quickly reached inside my bag, picked a notebook and a pen. I knew my day's lessons had begun in earnest.

"Success does not depend on what you do, it depends on why you are doing it." He started. "In fact, success is only 10% **HOW**, and 90% **WHY**. When we make a decision based on a strong **WHY** we own up to it. Only when we know **WHY** we do things, can we feel a sense of belonging. Why we are doing something is one of the most powerful ways of getting us to decide to do it in the first place. Once we are sold to the cause of an idea, we'll go above and beyond to support it with our time, effort and resources. And in some moments, even with our lives." He said. A soldier who has been told why he is going to battle will fight much more fiercely than the one who simply finds himself at war. He added.

He patiently waited as I took notes. I looked up and nodded steadily. I was following.

"When we solve the 'why' part of the puzzle, we are able to make the necessary sacrifices that will lead us to true success and wealth. You will need to make the relevant changes to your life like watching TV less, becoming frugal and reading or listening to information that advances you toward your set goals. The great philosopher Hippocrates once said, 'Before healing someone, ask him if he's willing to give up the things that made him sick'. I now ask you, he added, are you willing to give up the things that led you to that financial situation?"

"Yes." I quickly answered. This was both a confession and an affirmation. I had already made the decision for financial success over a $2,000 handout. I also knew that the mentorship with Mr. Client was giving me access to the practical and potent information that I needed in my life, but I was under no illusion that it would be 'abracadabra'. What I needed in my life would have to cost me something, and I was willing to make every ethical and fair tradeoff

 *"it's not just a book… it's medicine."*

so that I can gain financial freedom. With Mr. Client's guidance, I was sure that I would get there.

"Great leaders and companies naturally get this right. They start all communication with **why** they do things, then **how** they do things." He paused, pointing at the word he had written on the board.

"Please elaborate further." I urged.

"Take for example Apple, he continued, "first they tell us **why** they are here, then they tell us **how** they will achieve their why – their products such as iPod, computers, phones and tablets."

He crossed the room and went to the wall on my left which had a framed printout of Apple's Corporate Vision Statement. He pointed at the frame using the marker and asked me to read it out aloud.

It read, **"To make the best products on earth, and to leave the world better than we found it"**.

I started understanding why Apple is one of the most successful companies in the world; their WHY.

"Our lesson today is going about habits." He said.

"Why habits? I inquired curiously.

"Because habits are instrumental in the way we make decisions. And success is merely a collection of right decisions compounded over time." He replied.

"Habits are the surest way of transmitting information and behavior from the conscious part of the brain into the subconscious mind. Take, for example, new drivers. They do everything related to driving using their active minds. They have to think about everything, including turning on the indicator, using their active minds. It's not uncommon to see someone has turned on the wipers instead of the indicators. This is because driving is an active job for them. At this stage, driving involves a lot of pressure and many accidents are caused by such drivers. These people also get overly exhausted performing these rather simple tasks. But after several times behind the steering wheel, the driving habits start forming. Get in the car. Seat belt. Rear view mirror check. Side mirror check. Brake pedal. Ignition. Hand brake. Gear. All these seem to happen automatically. Why?" Mr. Client asked me.

"Because they are now a set of habits formed over time in them," I responded.

"Wonderful!" he exclaimed. "Success is a lot like driving. It involves moving from point A to point B using a set of habits formed over time. You might not be quite competent in the beginning, but with time and continuous practice, the steps become habits that become effortless and sometimes performed unconsciously. That is why people say, 'success eventually becomes a lifestyle.'" He added.

"Have you heard of the biblical saying that the rich shall become richer and the poor poorer?" He asked.

I nodded my head in agreement.

"Some habits will make you successful, richer and happier while others will make you poorer and unhappier." He went on to say.

"A story is told of a rich man who lost a big chunk of his assets due to something that was not his making. Some people were shocked to find him at the golf course playing his favorite game. When asked about the loss, he simply said that he knew how to make the money and he would still make it again." Mr. Client explained.

"You mean he had a set of habits that he could always depend on to replace the money and assets he had lost?"

"That's correct. Success is rooted in habits. It is seldom an event. Habits are the foundation of any sustained growth and progress that you desire in your life.

"Success is not automatic even though the universe wants everyone to be successful", I said.

Mr. Client nodded and just gazed at me as the truth sunk into my spirit. Finally, he spoke.

"The easiest and most obvious way for a Deity to bless his people, at least according to our perspective, is to perform a miracle for all of us. This is not something that is beyond him. But he won't do it. He has never instituted miracles as part of his plan and agenda for your success and mine."

I nodded my head in total agreement.

"However, there is something that the universe gives everyone—regardless of their skin color, gender or tribe," Mr. Client said and paused for effect. I then noticed that he wanted me to guess.

"Time?" I asked half convinced.

"Certainly" He beamed. "Time and chance. Another portion of the good book says, 'The race is not for the swift or the battle for the strong, but time and chance are given to everyone'. Therefore, the most universal method that you can use to be successful is what is available to everyone—the formation of habits that support your big 'why'. That's it. At least that's the biggest kick-start of it all"

This was simple and yet so extremely profound for me. This information was not rocket science. If anything, I think I knew about this, but I didn't consider it to be that profound. I always thought that wealth is created by special people with special skills. I thought that it is created by people who meet luck or who were born into it. My thinking was being challenged here. Mr. Client was obviously none of those who were born with a silver spoon in their mouth; neither was he that special in any way because of his back story. He built his empire by sheer determination and now I was having the inside story of how he did it. I could only be grateful that even as he shared the inside story of wealth creation, I had the opportunity to walk where he walked and succeed like he did—but there was a caveat. I had to participate in it. That was the greatest lesson I was deducing about the universe and success. It is to those who are willing and obedient that success would come—not to everyone. The laws apply to everyone everywhere. The principles do not change with a bias to anyone. And yet, to those who would apply the principles, to them the success would be bequeathed. It was a paradox. People are waiting on praying but the universe has already done its part by providing the laws and principles, the environment and the enablement. One thing would change people from their point A to their point B of wealth creation—their habits.

I recalled the poor habits I had. On the top was impulse purchases of items I didn't need. If anything, I didn't have any regiment of habits that were being coalesced towards a particular major goal in life. I was a lawyer at a progressive firm in town and most of my habits were centered around the practice of law as a career. Certainly, there were quite a bit of rewards in practicing law. I loved it. It paid for my bills. But I was still broke. My habits over the years had kept me right where I was—a needy person. It dawned on me that I lacked direction as far as financial freedom was concerned. It was a wish, a desire, probably a prayer. It wasn't a goal or a conscious obsession. Therefore, there were absolutely no habits to back that wish. Shaking my head as light entered my life, I acknowledged my responsibility in my ramshackle financial life. Wanting to learn more from Mr. Client I asked him a question.

"What has been the one habit that has been most responsible for your success?"

He smiled, reflected a bit and answered as he kept thinking.

"You know, I cannot tell you that there is one habit. It feels as if you are asking me for a 'secret' of sorts. Many people who seek secrets unconsciously do not want to put in the work. They want the secret to work—not themselves."

"How is that?"

"Tell me. Why are you asking for one habit?" I felt cornered.

"Well, I must say I just wanted to cut to the chase", I replied

"You must honor processes my friend," Mr. Client replied. "What you are seeking is not an event, at least, it will not come to you as an event. It has to be a process. I can understand that you want the answers like ABC or 123, but I have to warn you: Today, we have Google and Quora and many other search engines. I am 100% sure that if you looked for 'How to be successful' in any one of those forums, you would find millions of answers. Some of those answers would be right, quite a number would be wrong. So, you tell me, does having the answers guarantee you success?"

"Well, if you look at it from that angle, I do not think so."

"Then what do you think needs to happen for you to be successful?"

 *"it's not just a book… it's medicine."*

"Well, I think I have to put into practice what answers I get"

"You are doing life. You are not solving a mathematical problem. You are solving a life problem with some interesting and ever-changing targets. Therefore, the answers to life are not necessarily plug and play, there is something called context. The person living in the United States has a different context and environment through which they can apply the 'secrets' that everyone is looking for". He paused again

I was feeling a little bit lost in this lesson, but it was also slowly making sense to me. I wanted a direct answer as to what habits he had formed but that was not immediately forthcoming. So, I tried another angle for questioning.

"Isn't there one universal habit that all wealthy people play by in order to be successful?"

He thought for a minute and graciously asked:

"Do you think all the successful people want the same thing?"

"Technically, yes they do."

"And what would that be?"

"Money."

"And after they have the money?"

Before I could answer, he raised his finger as a professor would, to stress a very important point: "Clarity of your why is the most critical thing in life. As such, there can be no generalizations that can work in matters of unique and specific contexts. Not all wealthy people want the same thing. Their motivation is different from each one. The gravest mistake you would make in your life is to try and use someone else's motivation or motive to seek success."

I was learning a big lesson.

He continued, "If my reason for seeking wealth is different from yours, it follows then that what I do to get it cannot necessarily be copied and pasted for the success to be replicated."

Feeling enlightened, I countered:

"But we agree at least that all these people got there because of their habits."

"That's the lesson, my friend. That's the lesson. The question would be, 'what habits should I form?'"

"But that's what I have been asking all along."

"No. You were asking about my habits as if you want to implement them yourself."

"Well, I only wanted to learn from you and get a kick start"
"Do you see the folly therein now?"

"Yes, I do. Your motive is different from mine; I guess the power of clarity is important. If I wanted to have a net worth of $100,000, then my habits cannot be the same as the one who only wants a net worth of $1,000."

"There you go. However, if I was to give you one major habit that you would use, it would be the habit of planning, taking action and reviewing. Everyone successful does this and without it, they cannot be successful. The extent to which it is one again varies from one person to the next. Some people like Elon Musk can afford to work for sixteen hours straight. Some like Arianna Huffington couldn't because her body system shut down. She is now an advocate for better health as we pursue our financial goals."

I had heard of Elon Musk, but I needed to read further about Arianna Huffington. I made a mental note to look her up at my earliest opportunity.

"At best, my friend," Mr. Client continued, "What you want and the why behind it will be what will dictate your habits. It will also be what will dictate your work rate and your hunger for achievement. A man who is desperate for air is hungrier to be alive than a man who is enjoying his food at a steak house."

I nearly laughed at this analogy because it was rather sinister. At the look of things, one might think that I was the one gasping for breath while Mr. Client was enjoying steaks at the steak house. The difference was in our habits. He seemed hungrier than I was. He seemed structured, focused and consistent. He seemed like he had a True North locked and a compass to navigate life.

So, I was learning that my why plus my hunger plus my consistent habits would be the core ingredients for my success. The more I thought about it, the more it occurred to me that this simple formula was available to all of us. 'Time and chance are given to all'. I instinctively took the marker pen from the table and walked to the whiteboard. Mr. Client was a little baffled, but his eyes lit up as I wrote down what I considered my formula:

Why + Hunger + Habits + Consistency = Success.

Mr. Client rubbed his hands together and nodded as I looked at him telling him the summary of my lesson that day. He didn't even attempt to correct me or to add anything to what I had written. Again, he raised his finger as if to make a point:

"Context is powerful. I didn't set off to give you a formula but there you are. This is how your personality and perception has chewed the cud today to produce something contextual with you that you can use. You can now see how important it is not to copy and paste things. I love your formula and I can still tell you the same thing about context. You see, your why is different from mine. Your hunger is different from mine. I am not so sure about your consistency either, but I bet it would be different from mine too. However, all of these elements are needed for success. The variable here is the individual. How clear is your why? How hungry are you? How consistent will you be with your habits?"

"So, the ball is squarely in my court."

 

"Absolutely. In fact, something that I normally tell people after this first lesson is the same thing, I would tell you: If we added nothing at all to your lessons, this alone would take you places that a large percentage of people in the whole wide world are only dreaming of."

"Wow."

"Yes."

"Why do you want to be successful?" Mr. Client asked again. I knew I had my rehearsed answer but before I could regurgitate it, he added: "Take your time and explore the various reasons why you want to be wealthy. Make sure they are your own reasons – do not copy from anyone. These are your reasons. They have to come from you. Write the script of your life the way you want it and take full responsibility for its realization. If things don't work out, ask yourself why you failed, learn the lesson and change. If things go well, keep the passion, thank God and your team and keep moving forward."

I saw that Mr. Client wanted to bring the lesson to a close, but I had one question to ask him.

"If you are to give advice to someone about habits, seeing that they are integral to a life of success, what would you tell them?"

He smiled. "I can see you have not let go of your question, but this is a great way to ask it. Generally, the beginning point of habits that bring success has to be conscious. You have to be intentional about what you want to do habitually. This means that you will have to create a tradeoff between your current lifestyle and a new lifestyle. It is kind of like installing a new operating system on your computer. It is not a walk in the park. Many people try to do this at the euphoria of the New Year but shortly after the third week, they have resorted back to their default setting."

I smiled wryly knowing full well what he was talking about. He continued.

"What cements your habit is mental toughness and staying power. At very many points in your new habits' installation, you will not feel like doing it. That's when you realize that the habit you have chosen is the right one. It goes right against your comfort zones and status quo. The secret, if there was such a thing, is to have a great staying power. It is about exercising your will and your discipline more than anything. Take some time and study how Americans select their elite squads of the Navy SEALs. It is never about stamina or body size or power. It is always about their mental toughness and their willpower. Ultimately, you will know how hungry you really are when you must bank on your willpower and mental toughness to sustain your habits." He concluded.

"Habits must then be the core thing here, I can see, if that's what they do with the Navy SEALs," I commented sincerely, nearly tearing now that the lesson had connected to my spirit and that I was privileged to have had access to this information.

 

"The world of habits is enormous. In fact, there are very many books that have been written on that topic. You could read them for days on end and you would be inspired. In fact, James Clear has written an international best seller that I would immediately recommend to you. It should be your screen saver in your brain. It's called *Atomic Habits.*"

"That sounds powerful."

"Yes, just like the name suggests, small, tiny habits repeated consistently over a long period of time create massive atomic bomb-like impact. Your financial success is in atomic financial habits. The question is, what are you going to do about your habits? You will need to start some, stop some and improve some. All in all, habits that support your why are the way to go." He said with finality.

I was writing frantically as he spoke because I had lurched onto something. First, I was going to get myself a copy of Atomic Habits. Then, instead of trying to copy and paste Mr. Client's habits, I was going to do an introspection to find out the three habits that he talked about. Habits to start, habits to stop and habits to improve. When I closed my notebook and looked up at him, I was satisfied that I had so much on my plate to chew on until we met the following day.

We agreed to meet at 7:30 am the following morning for our next lesson.

I said bye to Alice at her desk and left the building at exactly 10:00 am.

As the day went by, I started being conscious of the decisions I was making. I continued reflecting even on the reason why I was working as an attorney. All of a sudden, my approach to life was totally different. I was not just existing and doing all that needs to be done, I was looking for meaning, substance and direction with my life. All in all, I was even more determined to add financial success and wealth to my life. I didn't just want to work for the sake of working and paying bills and surviving. There had to be something to life than what I was experiencing and I thought that financial freedom would give me a great opportunity to pursue a life of meaning. I also knew that I needed not to postpone this quest for meaning and success. I needed to start right then and there with a total mindset switch—there had to be direction in my life's pursuits.

That evening as I drove back home from work, my mind was deeply engaged. I do not even remember how I got home but thanks to the power of habits, I unconsciously navigated my routes and got to my abode. I felt determined to take a walk around the neighborhood in my sports gear to think things over. Clearly, a seed had just been planted in my life and it was quickly germinating. There was the danger of this seed being chocked by the cares that I had at the moment. I still needed the $2,000 and I had no clue where to get it in the interim. This embarrassing situation made me make a vow and to reaffirm my commitment to my financial freedom.

 *"it's not just a book… it's medicine."*

Back home, I set aside some solid two hours to do a thorough personal introspection of my life. The input in that two hours was simply about my WHY and my HABITS. I created my three lists of habits, generating so many embarrassing and useless habits in lifestyle, finances, physical health, mental health and even in my career that were derailing me. I then made a small but elaborate ritual where I burnt up the list of the bad habits while determined not to repeat them. I got my notebook and started documenting all the habits that I desired to pursue and inject into my life. Before I knew it, I was preparing a personal timetable that spoke of my entire life. Previously, I only put things in my diary that were work-related. I noticed that it was a bad habit already not to plan my days or my weeks, for in doing so, I was not giving my quest for success the wings to fly. My mind having been exhausted but my spirit thoroughly satisfied with the new birth that I was experiencing, I retired to bed a determined man. If Mr. Client would have charged me for that day's lesson alone, the $2,000 wouldn't have covered it!

## Practical Guide To Your Millions

1. Figure out the real reason why you want financial success and freedom. Without this, it is possible to give up. Clarify this to the details. The reasons you want to be successful must be yours, not someone else's.

2. Review your habits. What habits make you have a richer and positive life? What habits do the opposite? Create a list of your positive habits that you must foster and negative habits you must stop and existing positive habits you must accentuate.

3. Create an implementation routine/regimen for all your habits that you want to be installed in your life that will support your biggest why in life.



*"it's not just a book… it's medicine."*

# GOAL SETTING

*The pessimist complains about the wind. The optimist expects it to change. The leader adjusts the sails. – John Maxwell.*

## Wednesday

The moment my eyes opened early in the morning; my mind alerted me that there was something of a grand scale happening in my life. It is like everything had changed for me literally overnight. I was excited and at the same time scared about the changes that I will have to institute. This feeling was totally different from what I felt just a week ago.

Previously, all my focus in life was on my job and being the best that I could be. I had relegated ideas of being wealthy to an event somewhere in the future and thus life was a bit of rote for me. Today, everything was totally different. Life was beginning to be fascinating. It felt like I was a man on a mission and that this mission fully depended on me. I read about twenty pages in *Atomic Habits* and got motivated for the day. I couldn't wait for my next lesson even as I knew that there was so much to deploy from the lesson yesterday.

Stepping out of the elevator, I felt like a king! Time check: 7:18 am. Our meeting was at 7:30 a.m. but I didn't want to take any chances. I was already a changed man. Mr. Client had a strict policy about time – you are either early or you are not. Whether only a minute has passed, he would consider you late. Nothing more. He didn't believe in the saying, 'Better late than never'. They were merely excuses. To him, time is time and it needed to be kept strictly.

All the four walls of his office had clocks. There was a clock facing you, no matter the direction you are facing in his office. He had clocks for different cities around the world: Tokyo, Sydney, Nairobi, Moscow, Paris, London, New York and Johannesburg. I counted 9 clocks in total. According to him, they helped him keep in touch with his international business partners without intruding on their private time. He said the clocks helped him to know which people are still in their offices, and this encourages him to work longer hours – because as the day closes in Tokyo, a brand-new day is opening in New York. He had once told



*"it's not just a book… it's medicine."*

me the story behind the modern eccentric look of his office. He hated poverty and the looks of it—especially a poverty-stricken environment. For a man who grew up half his life in the countryside, this was a complete metamorphosis. His fortunes in life changed when his father lost his corporate job. As a young man, Mr. Client's father was a man of class. He had nice watches, designer clothes and shoes. He participated in sports, playing mostly cricket and rugby, a pretty interesting combination. In addition, he supported a local premier league football team that was in the first tier of the national competition.

All of a sudden, his father lost his job and that's when reality hit home and it did that in a tremendous way. Mr. Client's father did not have any savings to boast of. All his life in employment, he was always one missed salary away from hitting rock bottom. And yet when he got his salary, it was all systems go—he sponsored a whole football team, nearly becoming their patron. He bought drinks for his friends and they had a good time. Even though Mr. Client doesn't really remember how that life used to be, their family photo album tells the story perfectly well. When he looks at those photos, he sees the kind of clothes that they wore. They were chic, expensive and classy. They even had shoes on, the famous "Safari Boots" from Kenya. Mr. Client was around five years of age when the axe fell on his father. They were living in one of the most progressive cities in the country, but they had to retreat back to the countryside.

As it were, they outgrew their shoes and clothes and soon enough they were walking around in tattered clothes and bare feet. If anything, they were not even allowed to wear their shoes to the local primary school because it would make them feel special as compared to all the other pupils. Of course, as a young boy, he could not distinguish the two extremes that he lived under—one prosperous stint in the town and the rest of this childhood in the countryside. Obviously, his school performance was affected because of the trauma that he faced. He hated the countryside to the core because it was a 'bad place' as compared to the town life that he had a few snippets of. He had to make new friends and learn the local dialect which he hated too. His parents turned out to be extremely disciplinarian so much so that he could not dare miss a day of school. Even though he went to school, he hated it to the core. He was an average performer and soon enough, High School beckoned. He had lived in the countryside for over seven years and in poverty that by the time he got to High School, it was easy to make a distinction between him and the students from the well to do families. The initial part of his high school was spent trying to fit in and to prove to his cronies that he lived in a city too. His performance in school could not be kept at par with his classmates. They naturally seemed to be more intelligent and exposed than he was. He redoubled his efforts knowing that he needed to perform well in school in order to lessen the financial burden that his family was under. School was a project for most families, an answer to the scourge of poverty.

As usual, we started our day with a cup of coffee.

Looking at his cup, he asked me, "Do you know why I start my day with a cup of coffee?"

"No, I don't. Please tell me about it." I responded.

Mr. Client had a strict policy about habits, patterns and routines – he believed they are the focal point for all success.

"Patterns and routines." He said. "Rou-tines!" he repeated, dramatically stressing the word.

"I was hoping you would say something like the caffeine in the coffee keeps you awake and alert to work more than the normal person." Mr. Client chuckled.

"So, you mean successful people do not have some secret formula in their diets? I asked jokingly.

Not at all. "How are you doing today?" Mr. Client asked genuinely interested in my answer.

I beamed as I told him how I felt different like I was on a mission. I walked as if there was something of greater importance that I had to do. Mr. Client nodded in satisfaction as he took one more sip from his mug of coffee.

"How exactly is coffee helpful to you? Why does it have to be coffee?"

"Well, you need not read much into it. It could be just about anything, but the idea here is that I have that routine. There is a lesson in there which is a continuation of what we discussed yesterday, and before I could delve further, I would like to hear from you. Give me some feedback about yesterday's lesson."

"Well, I must say that it was profound for me. What you showed me was not anything complicated, but it was profound. I had never taken note of my habits and yet they were forming who I was up until yesterday."

"You mean today you are different?"

"Well, maybe not because the new habits have not been installed yet. Technically, I am still who I was yesterday because of the habits of my life all these years. But again, I am a different person because of the decision to alter my habits. I will be a more conscious person studying the meaning of all the actions that I take."

"Won't you find that laborious?" Mr. Client countered.

"I do not think so. I think the keyword here is 'premeditation'. If something is premeditated as we say in law practice, it signifies consciousness. If I premeditate my actions and decisions before I get started, I don't need to think about their validity as I am at it," I said, feeling satisfied with myself.

"I can never over-emphasize the power of habits. That's why today I started by telling you about routines. It's my routine to do coffee at this hour. It is a pattern. Again, it can be something else for someone else. For me it is coffee. For another person, it might be watching the global news, but there is a pattern at play," he added.

"Every successful organization is built on routines. If you set goals for you and your organization, the next thing is to draw an action plan that you and everyone you are working with will have to follow. The steps have to be so simple that anyone can fit into the system and perform just as well as the previous occupant of the position. That's the secret behind McDonald's, KFC, Burger King and the rest of the franchises you know. Routines are how organizations such as the large hospitals, the police and the military are able to train and maintain such large numbers of employees and yet stay disciplined. Sticking to a routine is the best way to execute your action plan to achieve your goals. All you have to do is write down your goals – personal or organizational – then develop an action step that is based on routines. Practice the execution till it becomes a habit, then your success will come automatically." Mr. Client added.

"But before we go deeper into habits and routines, what are your goals for the next one year?" He asked.

I stared blankly at him for a few moments, trying to come up with goals as quickly as I could. I always knew it was a good idea to write down goals, but I had never done it. I thought I could always carry them around in my head. Now that I have been asked, I had no idea how to respond.

"What are you currently aiming at?" He pressed.

I was starting to feel uncomfortable. No one had ever really asked me about my goals. Not seriously anyway. And, I had gotten so taken up by the legal work that I had not sat to write down proper personal goals to work towards. All I had was work-related deadlines. Those were driving me crazy. Then I remembered that I wanted to start my own firm. When I told him about it, Mr. Client asked me when I wanted to start it, how much money it would cost me, how many people I would employ and many other questions. I was having difficulty answering them because I had never thought about that one goal – to be my own boss – in detail.

"It is alright. Most people never really get to set goals – not in the proper way anyway." He said. "Today we shall learn about Goal setting." He added.

He walked to the board and erased the words W.H.Y which he had written the previous day and wrote the word: **GOALS.**

"Many people feel as though they are adrift in the world. They work hard, but they don't seem to get anywhere. One major reason for this is the fact that they have not spent a considerable amount of time envisioning what they want from life, and therefore have not set formal goals for themselves. Imagine setting out on a journey without knowing your defined destination." A small grin played on his face as he said this.

"Goal setting is a powerful process for planning your ideal future and motivating yourself to turn your dreams into reality. This process helps you choose where you want to go in life and helps you get to know where to concentrate your efforts." He added.

I started thinking about all the times when I thought I knew what I wanted; how I always thought that I had goals yet all I had were mere wishes. I had actually set out on a journey without a clearly defined destination. No wonder I found myself in a bad financial crisis.

## How to set goals

"Goals can be classified into three: the long-term, mid-term and short-term goals. First, you create a 'big picture' of what you want to do with your life and then identify the large-scale goals you want to achieve. To balance all the important areas of your life, try setting goals in some of the following areas: career, finance, education, family, health, relationships and fun.

Once you have set your long-term goals, next, set midterm goals (typically what you would like to achieve in five years) that will enable you to reach your lifetime goal(s). Lastly, set short term goals with a timeframe of about one year. Then break down these into six, three-and one-month's plans and then break them down further into weekly and daily action plans. Then create to-do lists — things to do today. In the beginning, these might be simple tasks like setting goals, creating to-do lists, buying books and reading them, meetings with a mentor or visiting the relevant authorities to inquire about business registrations if your goal is to start your own business. On a daily basis, you will have to plan, do and then review to check if your daily activities are actually pushing you towards your short-term goals. This is how you will avoid drifting to an unknown destination. Review and update your To-Do list on a daily basis. Plan-Do-Review, Plan-Do-Review, Plan-Do-Review! Do the same with your mid-term goals." He said.

"What do you want to do with your life in five years?" Mr. Client asked again, this time more serious than before.

"I want to be rich," I answered outright.

"That is not enough." Mr. Client interjected. "It is not enough to simply say you want to be rich. You have to put a figure on it."

"I want to accumulate assets worth $5 million," I replied. "Great! he exclaimed. Write it down."

"How should I write it?" I asked.

Then he pulled out his goal card and showed it to me. It was a small card – the size of an identity card. It had a date on top, and below was printed: I am so happy and grateful for the fact that I am making $1.8 million every single month. Wow! This is a huge goal.

I wrote down my own goal on a fresh page: I am so happy and grateful now that I have accumulated assets worth $5 million in five years.

 *"it's not just a book… it's medicine."*

"How about in one year, what do you want to achieve?" He asked.

"Go back to school to complete my master's degree," I replied.

Looking at me through narrowed eyes, he quickly asked, "How is the degree relevant to your goal of accumulating $5 million in five years?"

"Because I need it to run my firm." I started, "When you have a master's in law, you get credibility." I was beginning to understand how the entire goal thing works.

I explained to him that I needed my master's degree so as to run my firm effectively. And running my firm effectively would ensure profitability which would enable me to achieve my goal of $5 million worth of assets in five years. I would start my firm within six months and my one-month goal was to pay off all my debts. I felt like a knight!

"So, what do you plan to do this month? This week? Tomorrow?" He inquired.

"This week is for learning the necessary steps required to achieve my long-term goal of financial freedom. And tomorrow I am coming at 7:30 am for the next lesson." I answered.

"Wonderful! he exclaimed. You are such a fast learner." I felt good.

Our discussion on goals was pretty enriching just as our discussion was on habits and the why the previous day. I realized that one thing was building to another. First, you have the why and then the habits would follow. The goals helped you to put this big why into action. Mr. Client informed me how much it would be laborious to just come up with all those three categories of goals. As much as he was teaching me in just under one hour, he explained that it might take me the whole day to get this done properly. There were different approaches that I could consider. He instructed that I could consider taking a weekend off to just go and think about my life, my why, my goals and set up a strategic plan for achieving my why.

"That is the truth, but we seldom treat ourselves like we are an enterprise. It is easy for people to have strategic planning meetings each quarter or even each year for their organizations but never really do the same for their own lives. Isn't it amazing?"

I shook my head and hung it in feigned shame. Mr. Client smiled at my attempt in humor.

"Here is the kicker. For the most part, these strategic plans we do for our organizations do actually work! If we can have them work for organizations, why not implement the same on our lives?"

I realized that since I was born, I had never taken a weekend or just even three hours to seriously think and plan for my life and yet I expected an event to happen somewhere in the future that will culminate into my wealth! I reflected on the many strategic planning meetings that I had been part of. We talked of the goals for the year, the targets and so on. We periodically reviewed those to find out if we were on course or not. It worked for us. What Mr. Client was telling me made a lot of sense. I felt embarrassed that at my age, I had no real goals with a due date written down and being tracked. I was just existing!

"This is absolutely profound" is all I managed to say.

Mr. Client waited for me to say something more even as he appeared to study me closely.

"Does Alice have her goals written down?" I asked curiously.

"All members of my organizations have been taught what I am teaching you. There is an African saying that you can take the cow to the watering hole, but you cannot force it to drink water. I am very extremely interested in the welfare of everyone in this organization and they have been exposed over a period of time to this information and even more—for free."

"Wow. Do they appreciate it?"

"Some do, some don't. Others probably take it for granted but when push comes to shove in their lives, they will always remember these lessons."

I nodded in agreement. I was reminded of a lamentation a preacher had about his congregation that there were three groups of people in there. There were those who sit and wait to be served, there were those who serve and then there were those who are committed to the vision.

As if reading my mind, Mr. Client offered:

"There are three groups of people in any setting and you can divide them into percentages. There is a group that makes up 84%, then there is the 13% clique and then there is a crop of 3%. I read about this in the book *'What they Don't Teach you at Harvard'* by someone called Ian McCormack, I think." I leaned in to hear even more as Mr. Client continued.

"The 84% represent those who are just coasting around in life with no purpose and no goals. They simply exist even though they are paying bills and fulfilling their obligations. It is as if the noblest thing they do in life is to pay bills. The 13% are those whose hearts are locked onto something more than just paying bills. They want a better life and they have a semblance of what direction they want to take. However, they have no goals written down, no plan of action. Even in their existence, it was found that this second group on average did twice better than the first group, just by the mere fact that they had something they were looking for in life better than just paying bills," Mr. Client paused.

I had no idea which group I belonged to. At some point, it felt as if I belonged to the first group. Then with the input of Mr. Client the past two days, it felt as if I had instantly graduated to the second group. However, I carried all the characteristics of both groups in my entire life. The experience reminded me of the personality profile tests that people normally take. You are amazed at how at the end of the test, your description is so apt, and you wondered if you had visited a fortune teller that knew all your secrets. Clearly, I was more of an 'eighty-four percenter' than I was a thirteen.

"I am more interested in knowing about the 3% people."

"These ones are special for just two reasons. They have goals and they engage in personal development. Their goals are written down, clear with due dates and with a corresponding strategic plan for accomplishing them. That's it. They are very hawkish about their goals that they keep them prominently displayed and regularly reviewed."

Instantly, I knew that I needed to be among the 3%. I had a deck of questions that I wanted Mr. Client to answer especially concerning goals, but he had already said much. I was pleasantly surprised when he noticed my hunger for more information on the subject that he went on an unplanned diatribe:

"When you do set your goals, remember not to just have target goals or outcome goals. We started talking about routines today and this is how you embed them in your goals. Instead of outcome goals, you need to have performance goals. This will keep you focused on the areas that you can control. Your performance is connected to your habits and your habits form your routine. Once you have formed good habits over a long period of time, the habits will form you and will deliver the outcome. Don't go for the outcome, go for the process of growth that will deliver that outcome."

I was writing in a frenzy then it occurred to me that I could actually record Mr. Client on my smartphone. That way, it would give the teaching a better flow than the start-stop because of my writing. I asked him to allow me to record him and he smilingly obliged.

"What took you so long?" I smiled feeling foolish.

"Goals must be written down. There is pure magic that goes on in your brain whenever pen and paper meet. We cannot really explain it, but it is very instructive to write your goals down. Have a scrapbook that you can start with before you can refine your goals to clarity, timelines and actions. Goals written down can be easily reviewed. You have an opportunity to read them at least twice each day so that the imprint of those goals can be in your subconscious mind."

"What's the importance of doing that?" I asked.

"You want to live and breathe your goals. You want your success to be habitual, not something that you must always take time to bring to attention before you tackle them. That's how it will be initially but after some years, success becomes second nature. It is a habit, a lifestyle even. It is an automatic routine."

 

"Understood. It sounds really like work in recalibrating my mind."

"It is. Your secret is in the mind. You change your thinking and your focus and you change your mind. It has to be calibrated so much so that you not only believe that your success is a possibility, but that it is an inevitability. For that to happen, lots of doubt have to be extricated from your mind. That's why you must feed your mind with the direction that you are taking before you can open your mind up to the world every waking day. So read these goals aloud even as you think about them. Don't worry about this routine, whether it is working or not. As long as you are doing it, it will work."

He continued.

"That reminds me. The language of goals is always positive. Never negative. You cannot say that I don't want debt and set that as a goal. In doing so, your focus is on debts and not abundance. So, every morning when you read about debt, that's what you are recalibrating your subconscious mind to focus on."

"Makes total sense."

"Remember to be pragmatic about this and also to be realistic. Don't be evangelistic in your goals. Break down the huge operational goals into small and manageable pieces. The idea is to hit off these small pieces, chew them up and gather as much momentum as you can get. You have been taught in school about SMART goals and that's something that I can see you are aware of. Make sure those goals are SMART. It sounds cliché but it is extremely important. SMART goals help you with clarity and clarity is where your power in success lies."

I nodded in agreement.

"Perhaps the most profound thing I can tell you about goals is due dates. Every single goal must have a deadline. Nothing more and nothing less. The richest man on earth, Elon Musk at the moment, has been quoted to say something very profound about deadlines. I think I will paraphrase. He says that if you give yourself a month to finish a task, that's how long it will take. If you give yourself a week to finish the same task, that's exactly how long it will take. So, as you are infusing your goals with due dates, don't be too lazy about it and also do not be too ambitious about it. Be balanced. Perhaps you will know this in your own context because as you said yesterday, hunger is important and it varies from one person to the next."

I kept nodding.

"Life is about priorities. Goals are a way of forcing you to prioritize. A man with no priorities will never be successful in a million years even though his backyard was covered with gold deposits. To prioritize is to select between the difficult things that are uncomfortable but must be done and the easy things that sashay our comfort zones. Successful people have formed the habit of prioritizing so much that they are seen as snobs. They are not. They are just highly productive and their biggest asset is their time."

All of a sudden, he stopped and I knew that the lesson had come to an end.

"Again, if we did nothing else and you went to implement all that you have learnt so far, it would be more than enough," Mr. Client said with finality.

That lesson was sinking in every day. It was the idea that it is not about the wealth of information that matters, it is about the diligence in application of the scantest detail that you have that will count. I was more than grateful about this. I couldn't wait for the time that I would go away to have my first-ever strategic plan outside of the city. It felt exciting but also, I was apprehensive about the time it would take.

Mr. Client reached into his filing cabinet, picked a file and handed it to me.

"I have a case for you to work on. If you can get it completed by Monday next week, I will pay you $20,000." He said.

"Wow! $20,000. That's good money. But by Monday…" Browsing through the file, I asked, "Why only a few days?"

"One of the secrets of successful people is that they compress time frames. They attempt to do more in a shorter period of time." He responded.

Then he walked to the eastern side of the wall. There was a frame that had a printed quote by Elon Musk. I smiled because he had just made a reference to Mr. Musk earlier on. It read: **"Stop being patient and start asking yourself, 'How do I accomplish my ten-year plan in six months?'** You'll probably fail, but you will be a lot further along than the person who simply accepted it was going to take ten years."

Next to it, was a poem by Jessie B. Rittenhouse titled 'My Wage'. Mr. Client made me read it out aloud:

*"I bargained with Life for a penny,*

*And life would pay no more,*

*However, I begged at the evening,*

*When I counted my scanty store.*

*For life is a just employer,*

*He gives you what you ask,*

*But once you have set the wages,*

*Why you must bear the task.*

*I worked for a menial's hire,*

*Only to learn, dismayed,*

*That any wage I had asked of Life,*

*Life would have willingly paid."*

 *"it's not just a book… it's medicine."*

Monday seemed too soon but I agreed to the deal. The money was enticing. $20,000 would pay off my debts. Here is a chance of achieving my one-month goal in only a few days.

"So, what have we learnt so far?" He asked.

"Lesson number one was taking RESPONSIBILITY. Number two was starting with a WHY and developing good habits. And today we have learnt how to set GOALS and why they are important. We have also learnt that to be truly successful and attain our goals faster, we have to compress time frames. Attempt to achieve great things in the shortest time possible." I responded.

I felt like my life had already changed for the better. This knowledge was liberating. Had I possessed it earlier, I would have earned my first $1 million twenty years ago.

"Wonderful," he responded.

Then he asked me to study the case file and report back to him the following day at 7:30 am.

I left the office at exactly 8:00 am. Our meeting lasted exactly thirty minutes. I was already enjoying this. And now I had a chance to make some big bucks. My $2,000 problem was potentially gone. I went in for a handout, but I came out being taught how to fish for myself. I felt a great level of obligation not only with the case file but also with the implementation of the lessons that I was learning from Mr. Client. It felt like this was a chance in a lifetime and I was not about to let it go.

## Practical Steps to Your Million Dollars

1. Write your goals down and make them plain.

2. Categorize your goals into short term, medium-term and long term.

3. Create a strategic plan for actualizing these goals.

4. Ruthlessly prioritize your time.

5. Learn to compress timeframes as you take action towards your goals.

 *"it's not just a book… it's medicine."*

# PAYING YOURSELF FIRST

*"Do not save what is left after spending, but spend what is left after saving." – Warren Buffet.*

## Thursday

The first order of business was the case he had handed me the previous day. We kicked off discussions about it as we took our morning coffee. Still at the back of my mind, I did not know how long my lessons were going to last, and I did not want them to end. After all, they say learning never stops. All that mattered to me was that Mr. Client had promised he will be there whenever I needed him. That is all I needed for now. He had said the lessons were habits; Things that I will have to implement in my life daily, and if done consistently, will guarantee my financial success. To be honest, there was already so much that needed to be done. There was a lot of adjustments that I had to make in my life and every time a lesson came my way, I had to go back home and look at my rudimentary timetable yet again. Time was becoming such a precious commodity to me. I started to realize how that was so for busy people and even for wealthy people. Previously, you would catch me chatting away with friends whenever there was less workload at the office. I looked back and I now saw how crucial those minutes were in life. Of course, I understood that there had to be some balance in life. One cannot just be steeped into an extreme. With time on your hands and commitment to your habits, you were already on the path to success. I wondered what today's lesson would be about, but I was ready and apprehensive all at the same time.

"Success in any venture is merely a collection of good habits and routines, practiced consistently over time." He often said.

He had his week mapped out, Monday to Sunday. Most of his calendar was covered with work but he had time for every area of his life. He had time for friends, family and spiritual growth. Most interesting was the time he spent by himself. He curved out a specific amount of time during the day which he spends alone. He said this was one of the most important parts of his day when he locks his office and just meditates. These sacred minutes are not to be interrupted in any way by work. His employees well knew it. When home, he never checks his emails during family time. He switches off his mobile phone during mealtime, especially at dinner with his family. He goes on a dinner date with his wife every two weeks and takes the children out once a month.

When I asked him how he was able to start and keep up such a routine, his answer was simple:

"Discipline." He said, "First you have to decide what is important to you. Then make time for it in your daily schedule. Discipline is what will keep you going, even when you don't feel like it. Over time, what started as an item on a To-Do list eventually becomes a habit if you keep at it."

I nodded as I took some notes. This was one specific thing that I needed to implement in my life and I needed to do it immediately. To be honest, the discipline that I had was out of necessity, being steered by pressures of work and deadlines. If you removed those from my life, there would be no structure at all. In other words, I did not have the discipline to focus some time for myself. If my goal of becoming successful was pegged onto this habit, I was committed to doing it. I realized that I picked up quite a number of things that Mr. Client said in passing. I noticed that I needed to be alert and sensitive at all times. 'School' was not just where there was a classroom and a chalkboard and a teacher. I realized that if my mind was open enough, I could glean lessons in the presence of Mr. Client even if he didn't open his mouth. For instance, the quotes that he had all over his office were not just pasted haphazardly…

they seemed like treasure. He spent top dollar curating and designing those quotes. The way he interacted with Alice and the way Alice interacted with him was something to learn also. This man was living the life, walking the walk that he talked about.

"My early morning routine is sacrosanct to me. I wake up before 5:00 am every morning. I then meditate and say a prayer. Meditation helps me to become self-aware, thoughtful and grateful to the universe for granting me all my petitions. I am also thankful for the great things that I have not yet received but have absolute faith that these will come my way. The majority of successful people wake up very early in the morning. Notice that Jesus and Buddha woke up early to pray and meditate respectively. And priests and monks have for thousands of years have done the same." Said Mr. Client.

"Mr. Client," I began. What is the one discipline which you turned into a habit, and has had the most impact on your success?"

Even as I asked that question, I was fully aware of the gentle rebuke he gave me the previous day of expecting to lurch onto one secret as if it was the holy grail of success. Yes, I understood that success is cooked with different ingredients and the chefs vary. The motivation of each chef is also different. There are those that are doing it because they are passionate about it and then there were those who were doing it because they had to earn from it. For them,

 *"it's not just a book… it's medicine."*

success was determined by the pay. It turned out that I had actually asked a great question because it was specific about habits. I wanted to know the most impactful habit that he had run within his life. Naturally, I leaned in because I knew that what was just about to be revealed was a life-changing lesson. I knew that without this trait, probably Mr. Client would not be where he was today.

As if he had been expecting this question, he immediately got up and walked to the whiteboard. I turned to a fresh page in my notebook, so eager to learn.

He erased the word GOALS which he had written the previous day and using a black whiteboard marker wrote the acrostic: **"PYF"**

Smiling, he looked at me as if expecting me to ask a question. "You want to give it a try?"

"You mean I guess what PYF means?"

"Yes."

"I don't know. Passion Yields Fruitfulness?"

Mr. Client roared in laughter. I joined him because I knew I was kidding but at the same time, I also knew that I had no idea what PYF meant. People used acrostics a lot and the thing is that they could mean just about anything. The beauty with acrostics, which I loved too was that you could easily come up with your own and it could help you to remember things easily. Acrostics are also used as code words by some professionals. I had watched some anti-terrorism movies and was always flattered by the way they splashed out acrostics such as APB, ETA and so on.

Mr. Client loved a good laugh and he seemed to be wiping a tear out off his eye. He composed himself then wrote the words: "Pay Yourself First."

"I see it now," I blurted. I saw the words but was not able to connect exactly what he meant. So, I leaned in all ears ready to download the nugget.

"Have you ever come across this sentence anywhere?" He asked me.

"Yes, I have," I responded. Several times actually. Just that I have really never understood what it means. I mean, I am paid by our accountant at work. I am not the boss, so I don't decide if I should pay myself first." I explained. Mr. Client stifled more laughter.

With a brief smile, he said, "Not that kind of paying. We are talking about after receiving your paycheck. Who do you pay first?"

"When the month ends, the first person I pay is my landlord, then I pay the utilities — water and electricity — then I pay my phone bills. After that, I put aside money for transport and upkeep." I responded.

"I see," he said. "How about savings?" He inquired, "Do you put aside any money into your savings account?" He asked me.

 *"it's not just a book… it's medicine."*

Feeling embarrassed, I responded, "The money is never enough. By the time I am through with all my bills and expenses, there is hardly any money left to save. It is as if the money just passes through my hands and goes to its rightful owners. I need to make more money." I shook my head as I looked outside through the window.

"I understand." He interrupted my distant gaze; "Most people are in this same situation. They work every month, but they never seem to be getting anywhere. It is as if they are working just to pay bills and expenses. Many people fail to change this pattern through the months and years, and that is how they end up struggling most of their lives. Remember, from Newton's Laws of Motion – a body continues to move in a state of rest or uniform speed unless acted upon by an external force. Paying yourself first is that external force that you need in order to change the direction of your life. Call it a keystone habit." Mr. Client said.

"What is a keystone habit?" I curiously inquired.

"It is one which influences change in other totally unconnected areas of your life." He started. "When I started paying myself first, I became aware of where my money was coming from and where it was going. I developed a stronger will to stick to the budget. This enabled me to cut my expenses greatly because I chose to eat more meals at home. This in turn translated into more time spent at home with my family, and that's how we started developing happiness at home. I also needed to make more money, so I had to become more creative. I started a *side-hustle*. Consequently, I became more confident as my skills improved, and my belief levels went through the roof. Once I succeeded in the small discipline of paying myself first, I knew I could do everything else. I even started losing weight because I was walking more often and eating less – especially fast foods - only because I needed to save on transport and meals. As a result, I began exercising and dieting unconsciously." He concluded.

He paused and somberly reflected.

"You know, I have no idea how much money I threw away in my formative years in business because I did not know about this secret. I always thought that the most important thing in life when it comes to money was 'surplus.' That you need to have more than enough before you can save or invest. This lasted for years. Indeed, I made quite good money earlier on, but I only realized that I wasn't working for myself. I was working for other people. I was working to pay bills with the hope that after I had paid the bills, I would have some money left to enjoy. Invariably, that money to enjoy never really materialized. I noticed that even if I made more money this time around, the same problems would still be waiting for me. There would still be more months at the end of my money, no matter how much I made."

"Wow," I exclaimed. I knew exactly what he was talking about. I myself-was in the same boat.

 *"it's not just a book… it's medicine."*

"Paying yourself first is not a principle predicated on capacity or quantity. It is a principle of attitude. It is a cornerstone habit in that anyone anywhere can practice it. It firms up the discipline that we have talked about today in brief. The turning point in my financial success came when I started to implement this PYF principle. Of course, it is a game-changer but you need to understand that it is not an event. It is a process that is buttressed by a habit. When done well, this habit did the exact opposite of my previous life. Whereas I used to have more needs every time my income increased, I quickly realized that with PYF, I had the opportunity to increase the amount of savings and investments over time. It becomes a powerful cycle that when it is in full flow, it is a massive, massive support pillar to your financial freedom."

This was gold. The idea of a cornerstone habit. How one simple discipline could potentially change my entire life. I needed to start immediately. I was already sold on this.

"So how do I start paying myself first?" I asked.

## 70/10/10/10

"Simple. Out of every dollar you earn, pay yourself a certain proportion first. When I started out, I wasn't making much money. So, I would put 10% of my income into a savings account, another 10% would go into charity and tithing, and eventually, 10% would be for books, seminars and personal growth. I would then find a way to fit my lifestyle into the remaining 70%, even if it meant foregoing some of the luxuries I had been used to. Out of every paycheck I received, I would first pay myself 30%, then pay my bills and expenses last with 70%. Every time I made $100, $10 would go to savings, $10 would go to charity, $10 would go to my church and finally, I would have $70 to live on." He explained.

"Does that mean I should forego paying some of my bills to pay myself first?" I asked.

"No, no! he responded. You always have to pay your bills and expenses. I am just saying that you should pay yourself first."

"Okay," I responded, "Now I get it. Whenever I get a paycheck, I should deduct 10% and put it in a savings account. Then 10% for personal growth and finally 10% for tithe or charity."

Mr. Client nodded in agreement.

"And then what should I do with the 10% that has gone into the savings account?" I inquired.

"Don't worry about that as yet, we shall get there in the next lesson." He answered. "For now, you just have to take aside 10% of out of every money you make and put it aside."

"What if I am making very little money and 70% is too little to cover my monthly expenses and bills, what should I do?" I asked.

 *"it's not just a book… it's medicine."*

"Many people are making barely enough money to cover their monthly expenses. If 70% is too small, start with saving just 1% of your income. Use the 97/1/1/1 formula. Save only 1% of your income, then use another 1% for charity or tithing if you go to church, and finally 1% for personal growth. Then you can live on 97%. What matters is not the amount; it is the discipline which in turn will grow into a habit. We already agreed that good habits are the surest way to wealth and success." He said.

"The same way bad habits are the surest way to failure," I remarked.

He nodded with a smile.

I wrote down some notes. I knew that, unlike the planning that I needed to do with the first lesson, this one was a little straightforward and readily actionable. But even as I thought about it, I saw my 'disposable' income just dwindle immediately before I could ever put it to use. There is always some sort of safety when you have more money to spend. The saving was not something that I was used to and I knew that I would struggle a little bit to break my tight fists on my finances and start paying myself first.

"If you start by saving 1%, make sure you find a way to increase your income or to reduce your expenses until you are able to save at least 10%. Don't stop working until you can save up more money – even up to 50% of your income." Mr. Client added.

It made total sense. I began to wonder. I had all these things at my disposal, but I wasn't implementing them. Somehow, I thought that Mr. Client would pull the curtain off his immense wealth secret and show me how to make serious money. However, here we are learning about stuff that I should know at my age. I had every reason to believe that this is exactly what Mr. Client did to get where he is because I knew part of his backstory. He wasn't born into wealth, but he molded himself into it.

**How can you increase your savings?**

"Most people spend about 90% of their monthly income on living expenses. For these people to achieve any substantial change in their financial plan, they have to make adjustments. This involves both trimming expenses and expanding income. The challenge with some of these changes is that while they are easy to talk about, they are not easy to put into practice. Thinking and knowing what to do and how to do it will not get you anywhere unless you implement it. You have to walk the necessary steps for you to see any changes."

"Was it easy for you to start paying yourself first?"

"I did not know about this and so putting aside some money when I had been used to using it all and having full control of it was not easy. I had to break the habit and grow an incredible amount of patience with this habit of paying myself first."

 *"it's not just a book… it's medicine."*

"When did you get your breakthrough then?" I asked.

"It was when I reflected and realized that in the mode I was operating, I was actually paying other people 100% of my income. It was I who was making the efforts at work. It was I who was sweating each day. However, whenever the money came, it was others who were getting it. There would be my landlord and then the utility bills and tax and so on. It wasn't working for me at all! When this got to me, I saw instantly that I must not do this because it is just a good financial principle, but I must do it because I owe it to myself. I deserve this. It is actually non-negotiable!"

"With that revelation..." he continued, I knew that I had to work for myself harder and therefore, there were two major solutions. First, I had to increase my income at all costs. I could never be comfortable just working for others. Of course, life is structured in such a way that we cannot live it if we are not paying here and there. It is a paramount thing. However, that is not the main goal in life—living to pay bills. The other thing that I knew I needed to do was to reduce either the number of people that I am paying or the amount that I am paying them and then divert that money to myself."

"How exactly would you do that second part? How would you reduce the number and the amount?"

He smiled.

"I can see this got your attention. I am not talking necessarily about absconding and avoiding paying my dues for being alive, but there are some things that you and I can do." I was hanging on to every word that he was saying.

"Well, the short of it is one word: Adjustments. For instance, one of the people that you pay daily are those who work either in the transport sector or in the energy sector. The longer you travel, the more you pay. The more you commute, the more you pay any one of these. How about you make an adjustment and live closer to your place of work?"

"But then you realize that working in town, it is more expensive to have a house closer to town than further from it." I retorted.

"Well, nothing is cast in stone and nothing is perfect. If you took pen and paper and made some calculations, you will realize what adjustment you need to make. Either you spend less on transport and fuel and spend more on housing or you do both. If you are up to it, you will make the necessary adjustment. Here is the kicker: This adjustment will have a small reduction in your monthly expense, but if you are doing it for five years or so, it is a significant amount."

I nodded in agreement.

"As a matter of fact, you could make an adjustment on your house. If you are a single man, you don't need a two bedroomed house, do you?" He looked at me and smiled.

 

My house was like a treasure to me, kind of like a status symbol. I lived in an up-market neighborhood in the so-called 'Middle Class'. But looking at what Mr. Client was telling me; I was actually robbing myself with this lifestyle to pay other people. In order to keep my status, I had to part with lots of cash that belonged to me and willingly gave it to other people so that I can earn some respect, but at the expense of my life and my generations.

In a split second, I was able to see what adjustments that I could make. In that same split second, I had changed my outlook about life. I didn't need to pay people to please others. I didn't need to eat at expensive restaurants to prove a point. I could pay myself instead. I did not have to have a TV subscription and pay for expensive packages. Some of these subscriptions are just about getting one particular service such as the English Premier League. It was crazy to think that the rest of the day I am away at work and yet I had paid premium packages for my TV. I didn't want to go to the local restaurant or hotel to watch a football match. I didn't want people to think that I was poor. I wanted them to respect me because I had my own 54" TV and premium packages paid for. Well, the result of all that lifestyle was that I still needed $2,000 and had the nerve to ask a client for it! It dawned on me that I didn't really need that money, to begin with. There was no emergency. I wasn't sick. None of my parents had been admitted to the hospital. I just needed that $2,000 so I could pay other people in order to feel that I had 'arrived'.

I didn't need to do mindless shopping. Probably, if I chose to live a life of minimalism, I would eliminate quite a lot of things that I did not need in my life. I could even make some sacrifices and allow some discomfort in my life in order to create an avenue for paying myself. Seeing all these possibilities, I started shaking my head. I couldn't believe how much money I had paid other people out there for things that I really did not need and for years on end.

"Wow!" I exclaimed.

"I told you. The keyword here is adjustments. Once again, it is a personal decision. Your adjustments would be different from mine, depending on how much I want to be transformed. If you are OK paying other people, you will make few or no adjustments. If you loathe the idea of just working for other people, you will make considerable adjustments," Mr. Client said firmly and with passion. I knew from this that he had made considerable sacrifices in order to pay himself. He continued.

"It is important you adjust your budget first because if you don't, chances are you will start financing your lifestyle with debt. Avoid this trap. You may feel uncomfortable at first, but it will be worth it. You have to be willing to sacrifice a few luxuries now so that you can live like a king tomorrow. Be careful not to confuse necessary expenses with desires.

George S. Clason in his book *'The Richest Man in Babylon'* wrote about the seven simple rules of money. He wrote, *"Start fattening thy purse: save money' and 'Control thy*

 *"it's not just a book… it's medicine."*

*expenditures: don't spend more than you need,' as rule one and rule two. The importance of successfully living within your means cannot be overemphasized. Fortunately, all it takes is a few simple steps to achieve this monumental outcome."* Again, I was hanging on every word and jotting some shorthand in the process. Mr. Client proceeded.

"First, put together all the money you make in a month and the dates when the paychecks come in. Secondly, put together all your expenses for a month, including bills and when they are due. Thirdly, balance your income against expenses by trimming off expenses that are not necessities, until the total of the expenses falls below your total monthly income. Keep trimming until you have slashed away all the items that you can do without. Finally, learn the discipline of tracking – track every dollar that you spend, and everything you spend on. Put it on paper for review at the end of the day, week and month to establish your spending habits. As a rule, avoid "keeping up with the Joneses." Do not be tempted to compare yourself or compete with other people. Compete only with your own goals. When you start earning a higher income avoid the temptation to buy a bigger car or rent a bigger house. These  will only strain you and lead you to bad debt." He advised.

I nodded in agreement seeing that these things had already crossed my mind. It was comforting to know that we were on the same wavelength.

"What has been the most profound adjustment for you as you started your journey?" I managed to ask with curiosity.

"It was intriguing for me to track my expenses. It was in the era where there were no smartphones. The only available technology then was desktop computers with rudimentary internet that didn't have social media. I am saying that to tell you that the easiest thing you can do today is to track your expenses with your smartphone and an app." He paused and I nodded.

"Make sure you track all your expenses. The majority of poor people cannot tell how much they spent on which bills, and as a result, they cannot adjust their expenditure to prioritize saving and investment. The habit of tracking your expenditure will make you more aware of where "your money has gone" and help you avoid impulse purchases. Have you ever purchased an item and then after a few weeks realized you didn't need it? This is a common practice among middle-class families. Lack of control over your finances is a sign of carelessness and ignorance which are bedfellows of poverty. The universe will not add any more money to a country or man who cannot control and properly allocate the little resources he currently has at his disposal. The key to becoming rich is to spend much less than what you earn. Never yield to the temptation to spend all or more than you earn." He warned.

Animatedly, he added: "The apps today will easily categorize your expenses and you can see where the bulk of your money goes in a simple pie chart."

 *"it's not just a book… it's medicine."*

I nodded as I knew some of the apps, he was talking about but had never downloaded any of them.

Right on cue, Mr. Client kept quiet signaling that he had unloaded all that there was to give in the lesson for the day. He seemed tired as if he had worked the whole night. That notwithstanding, my mind had been blown away by this simple principle that I had learnt: PYF. It was a heavy hit on me when I realized that I readily paid everyone else thinking that I was creating a lifestyle only to realize that I was robbing myself to maintain a class. At the end of the day, there was nothing to show of it other than the hunger for more money to pay more people! I just shook my head from side to side, letting the lesson sink in me. A resolve had already been made even as Mr. Client talked. I had to be hawkish about paying myself. No longer would I be malnourished thinking that I was maintaining a class or a lifestyle.

There was a quick knock on the door as Alice swung in. "The marketing team is ready for you." She said.

"Thank you, Alice." Mr. Client responded as she shut the door behind her.

We agreed to meet the following day at 6:20 am. But before I left his office, he asked me to read aloud a poem that was framed and pinned towards the door inside his office. Untitled, it read:

*"Save a penny every day,*

*From your budget never stray,*

*When something catches your eye,*

*Fight the temptation to buy,*

*The future is only a day away."*

I said bye to Alice at her desk and left. As I got into my car, I started wondering whether I needed it in the first place. My car was a fuel guzzler and a seven-seater. In a month, I would spend a considerable amount of money on that car. Apart from the fuel and repairs, I washed and waxed it at exclusive car wash clinics in town. This happened almost every three days and at times, even more, depending on the weather. Was that really necessary?

That day at work, people commented that I was unnecessarily withdrawn and quiet. Some who cared thought that I was going through something and they came to ask if they could talk to me or if I needed someone to talk to. I allayed their fears, but it came to my realization that the seeds that Mr. Client had planted in my life had started germinating. My outlook on life was beginning to change and so was my approach and attitude to life.

By the time I got home, a lot had passed through my mind. Not only was I thinking of how I can get an extra stream of income, but I was also already drawing up a list mentally of all the adjustments that I needed to make. Some of these adjustments would be immediate. Some would be in the medium term and others in the long term. Whatever the case, the dice had already been cast and I would not be the same person again. I sat down and wondered about the house I was living in and even as I reflected on my day at work. After I had refreshed myself and rested a while, it was time to dig in once again and recalibrate my life. I took a sneak peek into my personal calendar and saw what I had done with my habits charter that I had created. I wasn't doing bad, but it seemed as if it was quite mechanical. These were early days and I was sure that with time, I would improve.

For the next two hours, I took pen and paper and thought through all the life adjustments that I needed to make. That afternoon, I had approached my banker and created a savings account that would not be accessed for three years. It was now time to determine how much of my income could be channeled to that account every month. I would have to prune my life to the bones to be able to actually save 30% of my income once all the adjustments earmarked are put into play. Sweat broke on my brow when I realized the monumental decision that I had just made. However, I was excited because I knew that for the very first time in my life, I was going to pay myself. It was a day of new beginnings. After this exercise, I determined to create a standing order for 30% of my income directly into my savings account. As I did that, I was forcing myself to speed up on the adjustments. I might have to sell the fuel guzzler and get an economically viable vehicle. Class was no longer an issue for me, paying myself first was now the mission. Eventually, I would have to move out of the expensive furnished apartment as I culled my life down to that of a minimalist so that I could pay myself first. For me, it was payback time. I had spent a considerable amount of cash-paying other people and it was time to get a fair share of my own money.

**Practical Guide To Your Millions**

1. Build a habit of paying yourself first.

2. Create a channel where your savings will flow.

3. Increase your income streams.

4. Create a lifestyle that will see less unnecessary expenses and more savings.

5. Dutifully track all your expenses and analyze them every month.

6. Create a budget and stick to it.

CHAPTER 5

# INVESTING LIKE THE RICH

*"Compound interest is the wonder of  the world. He who understands it, earns it. He who doesn't, pays it." – **Albert Einstein.***

*"Wealth like a tree grows from a tiny seed. The sooner you plant that seed the sooner shall the tree grow." – **George. S. Clason.***

**Friday**

There was a heavy downpour, but I managed to get to Mr. Client's office in time; 6:08 a.m. Surprisingly, everyone else was already present. The gloomy weather seems not to have affected the time of  their arrival at work. After our usual greetings and then a discussion about the case over a cup of  coffee, I asked him, "Does any of  these people ever come late?"

He laughed out so loudly seemingly surprised at the question.

"Yes, they do. Once in a while. In life, some circumstances are unavoidable. For example, if someone gets involved in a car accident on their way to work, or if their kid is sick…" He left the sentence hanging.

"I am listening."

"Life can blindside you at times. There was a season in time when my mother was sick. I had so much work to do I couldn't imagine not being at the office. At that time, I knew what priorities in life meant. I chose my mother overwork. When such things happen, one must have buttressed themselves so much that you have shock absorbers financially to handle the situation. So, there are moments when people are caught up in the throes of life that they have to either come late or not show up at all. However, they are motivated enough that when all things are constant, people show up to work early enough." He said with satisfaction.

I nodded knowing exactly what he meant. At times, I felt motivated to work so much so that nobody had to follow me up and ask me where I was and what I was doing. I was learning to be my own boss first and it proved to be one of the most productive and stress-free things to do.

"Our parking lot does not have titles. There is no reserved parking spot for me, the HR, the CFO, or any of the employees. The good parking slots are available on a first-



*"it's not just a book… it's medicine."*

come-first-served basis. Because of that, everyone strives to get here earlier than the rest. We also have a system where we post a picture of the day's "earliest bird" on the notice board, and then at the end of the month, we present an award to the person with the highest number of appearances. The competition is very exciting. Everyone loves it. But generally, they love working here. Everyone understands their responsibility and are committed to the company's growth and success. We work as one unit, so they expect everyone to be at their duty stations at all times. Our company is like an engine, every part working with the others to achieve a common result. A delay in one department means a delay in the entire organization and the employees know it, hence they strive to be here in time, regardless of the physical circumstances like weather." He said.

I recalled the numerous visits when I have seen his employees crisscrossing through the floor, like bees in a hive. Everyone was busy and they seemed to know what they were doing. This was quite the opposite of where I was working.

"So how did you achieve this?" I asked.

A brief smile played on his face. "Simple. You just have to figure out how to make your employees own up to the company." He replied.

"Churches, businesses, Non-Governmental Organizations, Schools or Firms are all built using this same principle."

Mr. Client began as he walked to the whiteboard and wrote the word **ROUTINE.**

"You will most likely face some challenges with your first set of routines in your first venture. Try to make sure you automate everything in your company so that they do not have to ask you for every small decision. I'm not saying you should be distant from the decision-making process but that you should simply teach your people to be self-reliant, not to be too dependent on you. That's the first step towards financial freedom. Treat every experience as a learning opportunity. Once you have succeeded in building your first organization, the rest of your businesses will grow almost automatically, and they will grow even faster. And with many  income streams, you have a chance of hitting your goals much faster than someone who is relying on only a single income stream." He concluded.

I nodded and paused for a moment.

"You have probably heard the saying, 'The rich get richer while the poor get poorer.' It is true, and only because the rich take time to learn about money, wealth and investment. Because of this learning, they think differently about money as compared to the poor and the middle class. They then go ahead to do things differently with their money. It is this difference that makes them richer. It is therefore of necessity that you invest heavily in your financial education because learning never stops." Mr. Client remarked.

I nodded in agreement.

"The easiest form of investment that you can make is in your personal education about wealth and finances. I tell you; it is to those who are hungry that the floodgates of this potent information are given. Otherwise, it is all over the place and people just stumble across it and at times ignore it. However, the foundation of your wealth is in your knowledge about it."

"How is that related to routine?"

"It is very much related. Routine is one of the most powerful things on earth. The sun uses routine, or at least the planetary system does. Each day, a routine rotation has to be made by the planets around the sun. Seasons use routine. There is summer, autumn, spring and winter. Time uses routine. There is a second, a minute, an hour, a day, a week, a month and so on. Behind every routine, there is an automation of things." Mr. Client paused for a minute to enable him to reflect.

'The question that you need to answer today is this; In your financial life, at least in your quest for financial freedom and success, what routine are you employing?"

I looked at him pitifully; knowing full well that up until then, my life discipline had been lacking, let alone my financial discipline. I knew he did not expect me to answer that question then and there, but it stung me to come to the realization that there was no deliberate routine that I was using in my life.

"Every routine has a building block and a theme around it. It is important to focus on those building blocks more than anything because they are the ones that will inform the direction and speed that the routine will use to revolve. At the end of the day, you will notice that your routine can easily be called 'Investment'. If you are unaware, you are investing your time towards something that you probably have no control over. If you are aware, you are investing your time and resources in building routines that will buttress you and give you financial freedom. The lesson today is not just about routines, but it is also about investments."

I was absorbing this information as much as I could and even writing down some nuggets. It was very easy to take for granted what Mr. Client was saying because he seemed so nonchalant about it. However, I had learnt to take every single detail seriously. I was indeed investing in liabilities rather than in assets now that he mentioned conscious investments and unconscious investments. I began to wonder what routines I had formed that were directly attributed to my financial investments. The only thing that came up was the savings account that I had created yesterday and the standing order that I was to issue towards it. I encouraged myself that the routines I would implement to reduce my unnecessary expenses would help in the long run.

"If you are not an investor, my friend, you can as well forget about wealth and financial freedom. There is no powerful avenue for financial freedom than investments. The idea here is that you need to create routine 'investments,'" he made gestures with his hands to show that investments were in quotes, "that will directly contribute to your financial freedom. Like the planets rotating effortlessly around the sun, your routines should be structured so much so that they are running when you are not there. That can only happen when you invest and of course, that is the reason why we had the lesson yesterday."

"So that I can have what to invest?" I interjected.

"Yes. Saving alone, even though it is ten times better than nothing, it is not enough. Investments are what kick that saving power into a noticeable routine that can start generating income and increasing your capacity."

I quickly wrote into my notebook and also made a mental note to start looking for avenues of investment, but then it occurred to me that I was in the very presence of the guru. I should ask him about it.

"There are two things," he said. "First, there is getting the knowledge. In fact, I would say there are three things. Once you get the knowledge, you can then make a decision. However, the third part is the actual investing and this is predicated on the capacity that you have built over time. You see, the rich work with goals in every aspect of their lives."

"They are glued to the goals in all areas of their lives. The decisions they make are backed by their goals – short-term, mid-term or long-term goals. That is why they don't stray away from their ultimate goal: financial freedom. Financial freedom is having more money coming in from investments each month than is going out through expenses."

I nodded vigorously because I had been cracking my head the previous night trying to figure out where an extra source of income in my life would come from. Today, that question was being answered and I was excited about it.

"Part of your income should be from your investments that come out of dividends from stocks, or from real estate ventures or from a personal business venture." Mr. Client offered.

A cold sweat broke on my brow. I was totally green as far as those things he mentioned were concerned. I did not have any stock options or even real estate. The talk of real estate kind of stressed me a bit and I mentioned as much to Mr. Client.

"What do you think could be the problem? Why would you feel that way?"

"I don't know. I grew up thinking that real estate is way beyond my league and that thought is still lingering in my spirit as we speak."

"Would you say that you are afraid of real estate?"

"I just think it is a huge area to venture into."

"I will take that as a Yes."

 *"it's not just a book… it's medicine."*

"Did you know that a fraction of your salary, which I am at liberty to guess can get you started in the real estate journey?

The entry-level into real estate is something that you can manage. Once you have your belief system updated by actual evidence, you can move a level higher and so on and so forth. All in all, real estate is one of the most powerful ways in which you can start generating income. Again, our time is not enough to cover everything that there is to cover about real estate, and I guess this is the point in time that the teacher has to give the student an assignment. Your assignment is to be as practical as possible about real estate. Get the information and get started. You are a lawyer, so I am sure you will avoid the many pitfalls that await gullible people that launch blindly into that space."

"I agree my knowledge is an asset," I said.

"So, as I was saying, investments should be the goal of saving. The more you can save, the more you can invest. The more you can invest, the more you can save. Once you get to the routine that is flawless where part or the whole of the proceeds of your investments can be re-invested, you are well on your way to financial freedom."

"Why would I invest all of the proceeds back?" I asked.

"Because you already planned and have catered for your expenses, remember?"

"Yes, yes."

"Those who accumulate great amounts of wealth use a two-step plan. First, they save part of their monthly income as we have already learnt.

Using the 70/10/10/10 or any other suitable plan, they put aside a specific amount of money each month. Routine is the key here. Then they convert this saved part of earned income into passive income. Choosing which vehicle is the best is up to you. Grant Cardone of Cardone Enterprises says you should not invest your money in anything which is a gamble. He strictly recommends real estate if you are a beginner. And you know something; I agree with him 100%. In fact, I would add that you shouldn't invest any amount of cash that you are unwilling to lose, and you shouldn't invest in something you are ambiguous about."

"Why would I be willing to lose?"

"Investments are risks that must be made in order to give us any form of return. When I say you should never invest what you are not willing to lose, I mean that you should have done the first part—setting aside the money for investment. This doesn't affect your daily living expenses. I have seen people selling land in order to invest in some new fad that has come to town. The question is: are you willing to lose property as you invest it into liquid assets?"

"I see it now," I quipped. "It is interesting that this Grant Cardone guy says that as a beginner I should start with real estate?"

"Yes, believe it or not. Of course, there are other options such as stocks which are moderate enough and again, you need to go and research about that. However, I would recommend that you get started straight away with your investments in real estate as part of your assignment. Countless people have succeeded in real estate, so it is easy to just emulate what they are doing."

"But why real estate in particular? Why do you feel like this is where I should start?"

"The first answer is this: Simplicity"

"What?"

You heard me right. I know you have your prejudice against it but hear me out."

"I am listening."

"Real estate investment can really be simple if you understand the basic factors of investment like risk. And it is quite straightforward: you buy or build, avoid going bankrupt, and earn money through rent. Then you can reinvest and develop even more properties. But keep in mind, simple doesn't mean easy. If you make a mistake, the consequences can sometimes be disastrous. When investing in real estate, the goal is to put more money to work today so you can have more money in the future."

He stopped to emphasize the 'future'. He explained that real estate is not like a job where you expect to get a salary in thirty days. The returns from real estate to break even can take quite a while but once that is done, the routine of payment from real estate investment would now kick in and deliver us from financial woes.

"There are two major ways of making money in real estate: the first one is developing properties for monthly cash flow in terms of rent, and the second is developing or buying properties for sale at a profit. Of the two, I prefer the former especially if you are a beginner and do not have the excess cash required to develop properties for cash flow.

It can help you multiply and grow your capital a lot faster, then you can eventually start developing properties for cash flow. When investing for cash flow, the money you are collecting from a property must at least cover your monthly expenses – such as utilities, maintenance and insurance – on that particular property."

A quick glance at me revealed to Mr. Client that I was still struggling with the idea that I could venture into real estate. He paused for a minute then said two words.

"Growth moment."

"I beg your pardon?"

"I can see the discomfort that you have at the moment. You are very comfortable with your life and you do not really want to venture out."

I sighed.

"How bad do you really want to get out of debt and into financial freedom? Do you remember your why?"

"I do."

"Then this is a growth moment for you. You recognize a growth moment by the fears that you face and the apprehensions that come to you. Believe me, it is part and parcel of your investment journey. I can tell you that what you are feeling right now is nothing but an illusion. When you have conquered the real estate mountain, you will be thinking that you could even have started earlier and that there was absolutely nothing to lose therein."

"Thanks for the motivation. Indeed, this is a growth moment for me."

"And here is the secret. The more you identify growth moments in your life, the more you are growing. The less the growth moments, the more you are the same, in fact, the more you regress." Mr. Client said.

"So do I have to wait until I have something tangible from my savings routine before I delve into real estate?" I asked, half stalling on his assignment and half curious.

"Well, you could do what brought you here in the first place but for the right reasons."

"You mean to borrow money to invest?"

"Yes. Actually, banks can lend you money to invest in real estate." Mr. Client said.

"I am listening."

"Depending on how you use it, debt can be both good and bad. Bad debt is money borrowed for non-income generating expenses like going on a boat cruise or vacation. Good debt is money you borrow to invest, and the interest is paid by someone else. Good debt can be a good place to start if you don't have a lot of money to invest. And the best part is that a bank can actually lend you money to invest in real estate, but the same bank cannot lend you money to buy its own stock."

I reflected on my desperation in asking for the $2,000 from Mr. Client. There was absolutely no income-generating activity that I was to be involved in. The most amusing thing was that I was so bold to ask for it! I felt a little embarrassed. My financial statements reminded me of the debts that I had taken previously. They were all bad debt! I didn't need them, looking back especially from the lesson on minimalism. I was living well beyond my means and using debt at times to finance my vanity!

"I see," I exhaled as Mr. Client explained.

"One big advantage that real estate gives you is stability. Real estate also usually offers a more stable cash flow. This happens when you buy or develop property such as an apartment building or office complex. Cash flow can also come from other types of real estate properties such as Office buildings, Warehouses, shopping malls and Arcades. When you have accumulated a substantial number of rental properties, you are guaranteed a steady stream of income compared to other investment vehicles. And in the long run, your properties usually increase in value, automatically raising your net worth. You can never go wrong with real estate seeing that the foundation of it is land—a commodity that is not being manufactured anymore," He smiled.

The more he talked about real estate, the more the ice in my life as far as that venture is concerned was thawing away. If I could dream, I could see myself owning property. My dream was to be financially free and if Mr. Client was prescribing real estate, then real estate it will be.

With these, I came to understand why most of Mr. Client's legal assignments with us related to the acquisition and sale of real estate. It now made total sense. I had seen quite a number of his properties and now I understood why he rated them highly in the wealth creation agenda.

I had heard more than enough from Mr. Client that day and I had quite a number of practical things that I needed to be done. As I left his office that morning, my mind was reeling with thoughts. Not only was I going to be saving as I had already instructed the bank, but I would also be looking at the option of investing in real estate, stocks or treasury bills.

Mr. Client had told me that time was of the essence, timing was important but so was patience, consistency and trusting the process.

With my notebook at hand that evening, I did not have much to write but a lot to think about. I knew that the information Mr. Client was giving me was in seed form. Certainly, there wasn't enough time in the morning to cover all that needed to be covered, but he gave me just enough to figure out. The rest was up to me. I, therefore, lined up as many ventures that I needed to do in order to acquire as much information about real estate and investments in general. The most important thing that I could do was actually learn in a practical way. There was no point in accumulating information without taking action with it. If our meetings with Mr. Client were to come to an end abruptly, implementing the few nuggets that I had learnt from him, would put me in a better financial state within three years.

**Practical Guide To Your Millions**

1. Convert your savings to investments. Saving without investing will not lead to financial freedom.

2. Start learning and creating investment vehicles. Consider investments like real estate which will earn you passive income.

3. Make investments a routine. Stay consistent and trust the process to build your wealth.

 *"it's not just a book… it's medicine."*

# CREATING MULTIPLE STREAMS OF INCOME

*"Invest in seven ventures, yes in eight; you do not know what disaster may come up on the land." Bible –* ***Ecclesiastes 11:2***

## Saturday

I arrived at Mr. Client's office at exactly 7:25 am. Dressed in blue jeans, a white polo T-shirt and matching shoes, I felt rich and determined not to live an average life again.

Mr. Client himself was dressed in a grey track and jacket combination. As was his routine every Saturday, he spent the day driving around town checking on his various properties and also looking out for which ones to buy. Today, he had offered to take me around some of his investments. He was excited and in a good mood. We talked a bit about the case he'd given me as we took our usual cup of coffee and then set off.

As we drove off in his big black Mercedes Benz, he asked me, "have you ever read *Rich Dad, Poor Dad* by Robert Kiyosaki?"

"No, I haven't," I replied.

"Rich Dad, Poor Dad is a book about the difference in mindset  among the rich, the middle class and the poor." He explained.

Then he glanced at me, smiled briefly, and tapped 'play' on the car audio system. The audio version of the book resumed playing.

We drove through the suburbs as the audiobook played. We did much of listening than talking. Then I heard a statement which I did not understand: "The rich don't work for money. They make money work for them."

"I have heard that statement somewhere, but I don't understand what it means," I said to him eager to learn more.

Mr. Client smiled. He always smiled. Then he said, "Many poor people say they cannot invest because they have no money and yet you can invest your time when you don't have any money. If you ask most people why they are

 *"it's not just a book… it's medicine."*

working hard, they will tell you it is for money. By this, they mean a steady paycheck that provides security. That is why many people go back to school to get advanced degrees to try and land higher-paying jobs and, sometimes, they don't even like those jobs but spend most of their time doing them – while the things they really love like their families are sacrificed because as a matter of fact, we all have only twenty-four hours in a day." He said.

This called my mind to my master's degree.

"The problem with this approach is that you only make money as long as you work, and as I said, we have only twenty-four hours a day, so there is a limit to the amount of money you can personally make. You may work longer hours, but you can never work the entire twenty-four hours in a day." He concluded.

"So, if the rich don't work for money," I inquired, "What do they work for?"

"Assets. Assets!" He responded while bringing the car to a stop at a gate. We had reached one of his luxurious apartments in an upscale part of the city. The net income from this property alone was enough to cover his personal and family expenses, yet Mr. client had a dozen other properties in this area alone.

## The difference between the rich and the poor

"Everything that enhances your cash flow is technically an asset. Anything that depreciates your cash flow is technically a liability. Is your education an asset or a liability?" He asked.

"Well, now that you have used the word 'technically', I could as well say technically, education is supposed to be an asset but that's only predicated on the idea that you will get employment or use the knowledge better yourself with it. At least that's how it has been structured."

"Well, whether it has been structured that way or not, if you can use education to earn an income then it would have been a great investment. The question is, must it be a job? Must the end of your education result in a job? He posed.

I kept silent as I was mulling over the reason for going back to take my Master's. I wanted to gain more knowledge so I could better manage my firm. Certainly, I wasn't looking for a better job. That was not my reason for wanting to take my master's degree.

"Assets can be investments or businesses that provide a steady monthly cash flow without much work. While the poor spend time working for money, the rich invest their time learning how to have money work for them. In other words, how to use money to make money. Working to build assets is a lot different from working for a paycheck. These assets then pay you even if you don't work again for the rest of your life. That is not to say the rich don't work. They do work. A lot actually. Just that they work differently." He said.

"How about you? What are you working for? Are you working for a paycheck or are you building assets that will pay you passive income for many years to come?" Mr. Client asked me.

"I am now working to build assets." I quickly answered.

"Great! He exclaimed. You are a fast learner. That's why I offered to teach you. Many people of your age won't take in my wisdom even if I were to give it at no cost." He said laughing.

I was not yet used to his compliments; despite the many times I had received them.

"How did you start your first business?" I asked him.

Mr. Client smiled as he looked outside the window as if to summon a distant memory. "It wasn't easy. He began, I did not have any money left to save, but I had read about the 70/10/10/10 rule in a certain book whose title I can't recall. The money I was making at my job was barely enough to meet my expenses, so I needed a second stream of income. I needed something that would bring in money monthly – just like my job – a second job of sorts, not a one-off deal. I needed something I could do around my work schedule, so I started searching for what I could do to generate some income. After some time, I found a group of adult students who needed a tutor. My teaching skills weren't great, but I decided I was going to learn on the job. It was time to step out of my comfort zone. The money was not so good, but it was an addition to what I was earning. That gave me satisfaction. In my first month, I saved slightly more than 10% of my income. After about two months, the number of students increased from three to six. I suddenly found myself able to save up to 30% of my total monthly income. After six months, I began earning more money from my side business than my formal job. I asked my wife to help me run the business since it had become so demanding with an increase in students' intake. Within three years our income had increased by 600%. I did not have a university degree when I established the side business but as it expanded, my wife and I employed qualified teachers and formally registered the school. Despite an increase in our income flow, my wife and I agreed that our expenses must remain more or less the same. After seven years of running that amazing business, we sold it to an American businessman at $1.8 million. This is how I earned my first $1 million. The Internet did not exist back then, so we had to do everything offline. But now with the internet at your fingertips, there are hundreds, if not thousands of ways you can create an additional stream of income. You can start a service business, invest in real estate, launch an online resource, dropship, host an event or get paid for a hobby." He explained at length.

## Multiple streams are a necessity, not a luxury

"For anyone who is striving to be financially free, multiple streams of income is not a luxury; it is a necessity. When you have more than one income source, you get a fallback

 *"it's not just a book… it's medicine."*

position in case anything goes wrong with your primary income source. First, you are protected against the ups and downs of the economy but most importantly, you can reach your financial goals much faster. Financial security is not having to rely on any one source of income – such as a job, business or investment. That is the reason it is important you create at least one or more additional streams that can generate you more cash. These can be either active (such as driving with Uber or Ori Rides Apps after office hours and on weekends) or passive (such as renting out your car during the day or weekends for someone else to drive as you sit in the office). Have you ever heard of the statistics that "Millionaires have seven streams of income?" I am not sure if the number is correct, but I do know that they have multiple streams of income. Before we reach seven, how are we going to create your second income stream?" He inquired but wasn't looking for an answer. He moved on explaining.

## Why build a business?

"In his book titled *Cashflow Quadrants*, Robert T. Kiyosaki wrote that there are four different ways people make money on this planet: as employees (E), self-employed individuals (S), business owners (B) and investors (I). Whereas true financial freedom is attained by those in the I-quadrant, it is the costliest to get into. This is largely because to be an investor, one has to possess what Robert calls the 3-Es: Education, Experience and Excess cash. Most people do not possess even one of the 3-Es. Some of our parents tried the shortcut: investing their monthly salaries in real estate: buying pieces of land and building houses. The majority of us have copied this from our parents and are trying the same route to financial freedom, despite the number of people above the age of sixty-five who are in dire need of financial support. Don't get me wrong. It is totally okay to follow this path if all you want is to get by. But if you are aiming at financial freedom – never having to lack money and eventually retiring rich – then you have to do things differently."

I was all ears. He glanced at me and I am sure he saw something akin to a ravenous wolf feeding on his nuggets of wisdom. Somehow this just excited him to say more, so he continued knowing that his words were not falling on rocky ground.

Mr. Client recommended a slightly different set of steps for a faster path to financial freedom.

"I would recommend a three-prong approach if you are to be successful and financially free. First, save part of your monthly income. That pillar is so foundational that I can keep repeating it over and over and never get tired. It is not about the money; it is about discipline and attitude. It is not about the amount. Please take note of that. And then again, once the discipline has kicked in, you will be obsessed with the amount. That's why you will learn to cull your expenses as much as you can."

"Noted."

 *"it's not just a book… it's medicine."*

"Secondly, use the savings to build a business." He added.

"Hold on one minute," I interjected. "Didn't you just say that we should use those savings to invest?"

"Indeed, I said so."

"Why then say I need to build a business?"

"If you revisit the definition of 'investing' you will realize that building a business is just but one way of investing."

"I see."

"The business potentially has the opportunity to give you more income which you can save and re-invest, and this is where the third part comes in."

"Aha?"

"Use that business as a foundation to build or buy real estate investments." He paused for a moment to let his message sink in.

"It all seems as simple as 1, 2, 3 but it's not that easy. There are many factors at play, the chief of which is you. This message can be downloaded by just about anyone anywhere, but you will see totally different results. The common denominator is the application the different people give to this direction."

"I hear you. So, 1, Save. 2, build a business, and 3, invest in real estate?" I asked.

"That's a general principle. There will be very many nuances to that and they will be contextual to every individual. For instance, I do not know how hungry you are. As a matter of fact, I do not know if this will work for you, but it is what most successful people use. It is not about knowing; it is about application.

I was hanging on every word that Mr. Client spoke and even as he continued, an inner resolve was being cemented even the more. I was making some decisions in my mind and some vows as well. Indeed, it started feeling like I was a man on a mission. I resolved right then and there to implement these three principles immediately, fully and unreservedly.

To be honest with you, I look back at my mentorship with Mr. Client and I attribute my success to that day. That is the day that all things turned for the better for me. Better yet, that's the day that I decided to turn my life around. I got a grip of the money game. I started controlling my money rather than it controlling me. My life fell in place like an accurately filled crossword puzzle.

It is through implementing his recommendations that I was able to become financially free in record time, starting with almost nothing but a desire to be wealthy and successful.

## Four steps to creating multiple income streams

Mr. Client noticed that something in me had changed. I was no longer pensive. He saw a resolute fellow. There

 *"it's not just a book… it's medicine."*

was an attitude that had been created in me. No longer was I struggling with his advice nor was I scared of taking a step. I was no longer hesitant but daring and willing to take calculated risks. It is at this point that he also changed his instructions as if he was going totally out on a tangent. He seemed as if he was talking to his beloved child whom he so wished that he would be successful. For when he spoke to me again, there was care more than professionalism, humaneness more than teacher-student or CEO-Subordinate relationship. I realized then that whatever he would say next was fetched from the deepest part of his soul, his very values. I, therefore, leaned in to listen, learn and absorb as much as I could.

"The three things I have shared with you are important. Those are like pillars in financial success. However, you will need structure. You will need spirit and you will need systems to use. These will buttress the pillars and before you know it, your life will change for the better."

By that time, we had inspected his real estate and were sitting at one of the offices therein with our water bottles in our hands.

"My friend, you first need to solidify your primary income stream. Income…" He insisted on that word so strongly, "Is the first bullet in your quest for financial freedom. You need several but without income, you can forget about financial freedom. Luckily for you, you already have an income at least every month. That's assured. Therefore, first and foremost, solidify your primary income stream, and make sure it is stable before you embark on starting a second stream. This will not only enable you to take care of your expenses but also give you an additional fund to inject into your new venture. Do not rush out to start on a second job yet you are still on probation or starting a second business yet the first one is still struggling to break even. That will be a very sure way to failure."

"I take it that this applies all through in that after I have solidified one and I start the second, that one should be solidified too before I move on to the third?"

"That's it. Be patient. Don't multitask. Focus instead. However, I cannot tell you that this is absolute. It is just best practice. If you want to multitask and you think you can do it, it's up to you. However, I would highly recommend that you focus instead of multitasking. Get successful in one and then start another."

"The other thing that you need to note is that you should be a person of value. Success and financial freedom are not a mechanical thing. The richest man on the earth today is a man of value. So is the second richest as well as all the five hundred people on the latest Forbe's list of wealthy humans. One thing about all of them is that they are people of value in that they find a problem that they can solve. That is exactly what you must do. Identify a problem in your community. Research, ask friends, talk to neighbors and local authorities, interview colleagues, read articles,

 *"it's not just a book… it's medicine."*

magazines and newspapers until you identify an existing problem in your community, challenges and problems that have affected even you. Do not go looking for challenges faced by residents of Alaska and yet you live in South Africa. Look for problems faced by people living in your neighborhood – people you know. If you find a problem faced by the people and work out a solution, then you have found gold."

"That's interesting." I quipped.

"The interesting thing is that the problems you will find in one location might be very different from the problems that I will find in the same location. There is a contextual angle to it because of what we are passionate about and our different capacities, knowledge and exposure. Nevertheless, you will not fail to find a local problem in the community." He paused then continued.

"Finding a problem is the easier part, but the most rewarding part is crafting a solution for it. The best way to reduce your learning curve is to find someone who has already achieved the result you desire and then learn from him or her. Look around for someone who has solved a similar problem – chances are they exist, though maybe not in your neighborhood – and ask them for help in creating your unique solution. The internet has brought the world to our palms, use it to your advantage. Look for a solution that even you the seller, would both appreciate and be able to buy. Now is the time to make use of the

10% that you have been saving. There may be numerous solutions to a single problem, make sure you choose the one that will bring you the highest returns with the least effort and capital. As Uber showed us, you do not have to own a vehicle to run a taxi business. Do not wait for the product or service to be perfect, just launch and then refine along the way. Plan-Do-Review!"

"This sounds like Business 101," I said with a smile.

"It is. Business is that straightforward to start. Problem, solution, market. That's it. And here is the thing. Once you have identified the solution to the problem, be sure to Market aggressively. No matter how good your product or service is, no one will buy it if they don't know about it. Now is the time to dive deep into marketing. The best part about starting local is that you can take advantage of your natural market – the word-of-mouth marketers – that already know you. Many people will pay for your product or service just because they know you, and many will even go ahead to give you referrals if the product or service is good.

Some people make the mistake of avoiding working with friends and relatives in their new businesses, especially in the marketing department. Don't be one of those people. Use your natural market as extensively as possible to launch your product. Make sure that everyone you know is aware of your product or service."

 *"it's not just a book… it's medicine."*

"Remember the wisdom of Jesus who over 2,000 years ago asked, 'Who lights a candle and places it under the bed?' Let the world know about you and your wonderful product. There are also paid social media channels like Facebook and Instagram that can help you market or advertise your products or services. These are extremely large platforms through which you can reach targeted audiences."

"Everything rises and falls on successfully building your first side hustle." Mr. Client said. "Do not rush into expansion otherwise you risk losing a lot of money in costs that could have been avoided. Rather let the business expand on its own. And if you feel like you have exhausted the growth available to this particular project, then you can just go back to step 2 and build another income stream." He added.

"You mean step 2 of the 3, the ones about saving, building a business and investing in real estate?" I enquired.

"Yes."

"What about someone who has no job or business in the first place?" I inquired.

"If you have no primary source of income," he started, "just go straight to number 2 and you can easily build a successful business from scratch – with minimal capital. When building up a business, it is important that you create situations where you and your team members celebrate wins frequently. These small wins make all the difference between successful and unsuccessful entrepreneurs. Small wins such as breaking through with research, getting an office, launching the company website, first client or first testimony are all avenues for you to celebrate with the team. These wins, coupled with constantly rewarding your team, will fuel everyone to work towards the bigger wins." He concluded.

I listened attentively and deduced that there was no limit to the number of financial streams that one can set up. It seemed to me like that was a great key in financial freedom, but then again, nearly everything that Mr. Client had told me was a key. Multiple streams of income need to be a mainstay in one's life.

We continued touring Mr. Client's business interests and real estate setups even as he continued giving me more nuggets. There is something about being taught in theory and actually seeing the practical application of that theory in real life. Each one of Mr. Client's setups had a story behind it. He took some time to explain the origin of each of his ventures as we toured. He basically opened up and was vulnerable enough to tell me how they all came to be. In all of the stories detailing each individual set-up, there was nothing new from the lessons he was teaching me. The only thing I saw is that this man was hungry, determined, committed, resilient, daring and urgent with his work. My respect for Mr. Client went several notches higher but that did not thaw away our relationship. He was open to me and I to him. One of the things that I was so grateful for was

   *"it's not just a book… it's medicine."*

the privilege to be on this tour as the main man detailed to me how his empire was built. I realized that there was no major secret. It was exactly the things that he was sharing with me.

## Practical Guide To Your Millions

1. Consolidate your main income stream before building the next one. Repeat the process.

2. Build a business from your savings.

3. Identify a problem, offer a solution and market the solution.

4. Keep building other streams of income as much as you can.

*"it's not just a book… it's medicine."*

# PROTECTING YOUR WEALTH

*"A list of true wealth assets would likely include family, friends, education, talents, experience, connection to community, self-esteem, the ability to help others, and good health. All of these wealth assets contribute to an overall personal sense of well-being. It also includes the ability to earn more money and to be at peace with your inner self." – Dr. Lucas D. Shallua.*

*"The wise learn from the mistakes of others, it's only the fool that wants to make their own mistakes." – Tony Gaskins.*

It was 3:30 pm, and we had not yet had lunch. The tour had been wonderful. As his lawyer, I knew about many of his properties but had never been there in person. After the tour, I realized how wealthy Mr. Client truly is.

Being in the vicinity, he asked me, "Have you ever had lunch at a fancy exclusive restaurant?"

"I have had breakfast, I responded, But not lunch."

"Would you love to try out their food today?" Mr. Client asked me.

"Absolutely. That would be amazing." I immediately responded.

We drove in, found a parking slot then went into the resort. As we were ushered into the restaurant, I realized that almost all the waiters and waitresses were greeting him by name, excited to see him. He must be a regular guest here, I thought.

The moment we were seated, he asked me, "What would you love to eat?"

"Something simple," I responded casually.

"Really? wouldn't you want to try something out of the box?" he objected.

"Alright, I said with a child's smile, I will have Japanese."

"Great!" he exclaimed and we placed our orders.

I had successfully handled most of Mr. Client's legal work including drafting his Will, yet he had never asked me about my personal or professional life. Mr. Client had found

   *"it's not just a book… it's medicine."*

out about me off the internet while searching for corporate lawyers in my city. When we finally met in person, I asked him how and why he had chosen to work with our law firm. His answer baffled me at the time. "I read half your profile and liked your name." He had responded. And just like that, he felt convinced that I would solve an urgent legal problem he was facing. As we waited for our food to be served, I kept pondering on how a successful businessman of his caliber, with forty years' experience, could use search criteria to choose a lawyer for an important assignment.

"Tell me about yourself," Mr. client asked.

"I had a great childhood… and was one of the worst-performing students for a while. I repeated several classes but later became one of the best students in my country. I tested both extreme failure and success very early in my life…" I started as we waited for our orders.

"Great, that makes the two of us. No wonder the universe led me to you! Mr. Client shouted excitedly.

Then he asked me, "Do you know how my business partner in New Zealand has been able to build a net worth of up to $10 billion?"

"He has been lucky". I quickly whispered as if I did not want anyone else to hear me.

Mr. Client smiled.

"Luck, my friend, he said, is an 'illusion.'"

"How then has he built this empire?" I asked.

"Using the same principles that you are currently learning." Mr. Client replied.

I paused and looked at him. I actually stared at him for a moment.

"Are you saying the very principles you are teaching me can make me become a billionaire? That if I find out where I am, discover my WHY, set goals, start saving, then invest my savings in a business or real estate, I can become a billionaire?" I inquired twisting my eyebrows.

Mr. Client smiled.

"It's not as easy as that – but yes – you can become a billionaire." He responded.

"If it is that simple, why don't we have more billionaires?" I asked.

"Two things". Mr. Client began. "Number one; it takes time and not many people are willing to be that patient. And two; because of what you are going to learn next. What you have learnt so far can make you rich, but what you will learn next is how you will stay rich. Many people have failed to get it right, and that's the reason you hear many stories about collapsing economic empires. It is because they have failed to grasp that one simple concept." He paused.

"And what is that?" I asked.

   *"it's not just a book… it's medicine."*

"How to protect their wealth." He said, with a small grin.

"Imagine a storekeeper who after a very successful day of business goes home without closing and locking his shop thus allowing thieves to come in during the night and steal from the shop. The following day the trader comes back and conducts business but the same happens again – thieves come into the shop at night and steal from him. This goes on for months and eventually years. Will this trader ever get rich?" He asked me.

"No, he won't," I answered.

"And why won't he?" Mr. Client asked me.

"Because much as he is making money, he has failed to stop the thieves. So, he loses all the money he makes." I replied.

"Aha!" he exclaimed. "Have you ever heard about a poor man who was sued for $10 million?" He asked rhetorically. "Never! No one sues a poor man. The same way no one steals from someone who has nothing. But as long as you have started accumulating wealth, many people including the government will come for a bit of it. Those who are not prepared to deal with them – those who haven't protected their wealth – often lose. And that is why many people's economic empires crumble." He explained still smiling;

"The long-term goals of wealthy people rotate around both building and maintaining wealth. Accumulating wealth is not enough. Whether you are careful or not, that wealth can quickly become vulnerable to seizure or loss. It takes years to build wealth, but only a few days to lose it all." He said.

"It sounds really cruel."

"Well, but it is true. It happens all the time."

I felt like I had graduated to the bracket of those who are wealthy and need to stay wealthy even though I was not there yet. My mind however had changed. I did not see myself the same anymore. I was therefore interested in knowing how to protect my empire when it comes, or when I build it.

"So, what strategies can you use to protect your wealth from those risks?" I inquired.

"I am glad you asked, and to be honest with you, I think you already know most of these strategies. You have helped me with nearly all of them." He smiled.

My eyes grew as big as bugs. My approach to work was just to work as a lawyer. I didn't know that the same thing I was doing for Mr. Client I could actually apply in my own life.

"Just so we are on the same page, let me tell you some of the things that you can do to protect your wealth. First of all, you have to move away from yourself and create business entities. In law, as you would know, a business is an entity that is separate and legal in and of itself." He offered.

"There are several types of business entities that you can use for asset protection ranging from corporations, limited liability companies to partnerships and trusts. Depending on the country you are in, most of these entities provide Asset- Protection through limited liability accorded to its officers, directors and shareholders. Corporate principles also have no personal liability for corporate debt, breaches of contract or personal injuries to third parties caused by the business, employees or agents. Some of these entities also come with tax incentives that you, as a businessman, can exploit."

As a lawyer, I knew all that Mr. Client was talking about. I had done all these things for him at some point but today, they became real and relevant.

"That's where you come in my friend. You have been helping me with this stuff. I think anyone who needs to protect their assets will need to make sure that they get legal advice." He looked at me and chuckled.

I smiled looking at the irony of the moment, Mr. Client explaining to me why I was his lawyer and yet I had never used the knowledge that I had in Law to protect any of my properties, however small they might be.

"The second thing," he added quickly, "You need to learn to diversify and separate your assets. The idea of putting all your eggs in one basket is not wise, common sense would tell you that."

I leaned in because I knew this was important.

"Always separate your assets, especially business from personal. When you put your business and personal assets under the same umbrella, you are exposing them to unnecessary risk, a risk that can be avoided." I nodded knowing exactly what he meant and seeing exactly how I would do the same going forward.

"Secondly, separate your business accounts and assets if you have more than one business. Make sure each business operates independently and keeps its own books of accounts. This will protect the assets owned by the other businesses, should one business get into trouble."

"Why is that important?" I asked.

"You always want clarity and focus. When you mix your businesses like pudding, you won't be able to track some individual financial aspects of those different businesses. Besides, if you wanted one stream of business to grow, you need it separated so that its different nuances are catered for. The more you separate and have clarity in your businesses, the much, much better. There are people who have had their businesses collapse because they are looking at one figure of their entire interests and ignoring the little details that can be critical. Details are important. It is the cents that build the dollars."

"Interesting," I murmured.

 *"it's not just a book… it's medicine."*

There was a bit of silence as he let that point sink in. After a little while, he continued.

"One thing that you should always remember is this: use proper contracts and procedures."

"That's the third thing to do to protect yourself, I presume?"

"Yes, it is. Sometimes we do business in a rush and fail to execute proper contracts and agreements. Do not fall victim to this. Make sure you draw proper contracts for all your transactions, with clearly spelt terms and conditions. Do not rely on implied terms or relationships, use proper procedures and make sure everything is set up professionally. Always make sure the contracts somehow indicate that your personal assets are not in any way at any risk in the event of your non-performance of the contract."

"The fourth thing is about debt. Use debt sparingly. We have already talked about this briefly. You have to be absolutely careful about debt and use it sparingly."

I nodded remembering the stories that were doing rounds in the mainstream media about the national assets being taken over by a foreign country because of the country's national debt. I also felt a tinge of shame because I had wanted to get into debt while seeking help from Mr. Client for something that was not that important.

"One mistake many people make is to jump at any opportunity to borrow. Just because a bank calls and says you qualify for a loan doesn't mean you have to take the loan.

Only borrow if you have to, but most importantly with a solid plan to pay it back. Over the years, I have developed a strict policy not to borrow for anything other than an investment that will generate cash flow immediately. The streets are flooded with stories of people who have lost property because they failed to pay back seemingly simple loans. Keeping your property out of a bank's loan book as security is key in protecting it."

This was a strong point. In my work, I had seen several people lose their cars, houses and land because of debts to banks. Stories of business moguls who lost their glory and their assets to the auctioneer were all over the press. I had seen the pain in their eyes and the shame in their face when such things happened. I had been in mediation several times to avert some of these crises and for the most part, we never succeeded if the client was not able to pay or provide a solid plan that would repay the debt. It was shocking how many people lost their property and when that happened, their health was affected. Some died miserably and yet they were once wealthy. They simply failed to protect their wealth by taking unnecessary debts.

Mr. Client shared several stories of people that had been affected by this. I could almost see a tear in his eyes as he recounted about how a close friend had taken debt and lost all his businesses and property. What bothered Mr. Client the most is that his friend did not take counsel and had no business taking the loan in the first place.

 *"it's not just a book… it's medicine."*

After a brief silence, Mr. Client resumed his lesson with renewed vigor, as if he wanted to save me from the perils of being unprotected while seeking financial freedom.

"How many points have we covered so far?" he asked.

"Four."

"Good student. Number five. Please, if you have to get anything today, get this. Asset insurance is one of the greatest ways to protect your growing empire. Asset protection insurance is designed to protect your assets such as your car or house in case you need additional coverage surpassing the one provided by traditional policies. The main purpose is to cover the gap between the present market value and the original invoice price of the property in case of an unexpected event. Furthermore, this type of insurance protects your property when a legal judgment surpasses your existing insurance coverage. Consult with your insurance agent for more clarity."

"Makes total sense." I quipped.

"Still speaking of insurance, one more thing you must do is look at Liability insurance. This is designed to help protect you or your business from covered losses. It covers claims that your business caused bodily injury or property damage to someone else or their belongings. It also covers your legal costs and judgments if a client sues your business for errors or omissions arising in your professional services. If personally identifiable information is stolen from your business, data breach insurance can help you respond accordingly. Your insurance agent will give you more light regarding your personal situation."

"Very few poor people get sued," I added chuckling.

"People will always look for as many loopholes as possible to get some of your money when you become wealthy. You might be innocent, but they might use the law of the day to extract money from you. At times, you might not have control over this at all."

"That's why the sixth thing that you need to do is important too.

You need to have a diligent spirit. Nothing beats due diligence. Avoid rushing through agreements, contracts and deals without doing background checks. Ask around, research, google etc. before concluding a deal. An inquiry to a stranger may just save you a fortune."

Mr. Client pointed to a sign that read, CARS PARKED AT OWNER'S RISK. "This simple sign could absolve and exonerate you in case a car is stolen from your facility. Work with your attorney to come up with all relevant signs to place at your premises. They may just save you thousands of dollars, if not millions in case anything goes wrong."

For the life of me, I could swear that Mr. Client was particularly more passionate about protecting his wealth than he even was about creating it. He seemed more impassioned when sharing these lessons with me even as we ate. I kind of felt like perhaps this was one of the biggest tools that Mr. Client was using to build his wealth empire. I took special note of that as I reflected once more on some of my clients who had lost their empires by not going the extra mile to put up bulwarks to protect them. They were apparently more interested in creating wealth than protecting it. Of course, they were good at wealth creation but that alone was not enough to build them the successful business empires. This discussion was rather intriguing.

I realized we had finished eating hours ago and the sun had nearly set. I glanced at my watch: 6:38 pm. I had certainly enjoyed these past four hours. I was in a different world and was so drawn to it that I wanted to remain there. Physically and emotionally, I even felt invincible.

"I have had such a good time investing the day with you. Would you like to have another day like this?" He asked.

Are you kidding me? I would clear my schedule for the month if it meant spending every day with Mr. Client. I was learning so much in a very short time. I felt successful already. I wanted to learn more for I knew there was more. Certainly, there had to be more.

"Yes!" I almost shouted, "I would love to."

He asked Andrew, the waiter, for a pen and a piece of paper, and on one side he wrote his home address.

"Dinner is at 6:00 pm. I know you won't be late." He said with a grin.

"Sure "I responded with an even bigger smile. "I won't be late."

He said bye to almost everyone as we left the restaurant. As we were driving off, we made small talks about the weather, the economy and his cars. He had quite a number of them. He promised to show them to me the following day.

"Good night and see you tomorrow." He called out as he drove off.

I stared still at his car until it disappeared. Then went home. All of a sudden, I felt this responsibility upon my shoulders to do something with the information that I was receiving from Mr. Client. It was scary but at the same time, it was very inspiring and I was certainly up for it. There is something about being in the environment of the successful. Something about rubbing shoulders with the affluent. It could scare you but if your host treats you like one of them, you start feeling like one of them. In fact, you start seeing yourself as if you belong to the affluent. Now that the attitude towards wealth has changed inside of you, you have to make sure that it is not just a spiritual thing, but that feeling is validated with reality. The reality had to be worked on and already I had been given more than enough data that would be a fine blueprint for my financial success and freedom. My resolve kept deepening each day I met Mr. Client but now something had changed inside of me. I was feeling like a success and acting like one. I noticed that all my decisions were now channeled through the filter of that feeling. It somehow started becoming easier to cull the unnecessary expenses that I was struggling with.

## Practical Guide To Your Millions

1. Protect your wealth with more diligence than you made it.

2. Diversify your assets.

3. Separate your different business entities.

4. Insure as much as you can.

5. Do due diligence, nitpicking all contracts before signing.

6. Indemnify yourself.

*"it's not just a book… it's medicine."*

**CHAPTER**

# ENEMIES OF SUCCESS

*"If you know the enemy and know yourself, you need not fear the result of battles. If you know yourself but not the enemy, for every victory gained you will also suffer a defeat. If you know neither the enemy nor thyself, you will succumb in every battle."* – **Sun Tzu, The Art of War.**

*"God loves you but don't dance with the lion."* – **African proverb.**

All along, I had been receiving doses of nuggets on wealth creation from Mr. Client in the mornings. Saturday was a different treat. It felt like I was on a full-fledged retreat. The only difference is that this was not announced and so my mind was not thinking like it was a retreat. However, what I learnt that Saturday was so much packed with practical examples and a live demonstration of the products of these principles that he was sharing with me. As I reflected, I realized that Mr. Client might not have necessarily called this a lesson but the fact that he dwelt on success and its enemies meant that it was an important aspect of life that I needed to be fully aware of and take note of.

In the evening back at home, I started remembering his admonition and prepared myself some notes.

I couldn't stop thinking about the day - how we had toured Mr. Client's various investments. How could a man gather so much wealth with so much happiness along with it? Most people were either rich or happy, not both. I definitely wanted to be like him — rich, respected and happy, yet so unassuming.

During our daytime drive, he also taught me about some of the other reasons people never really become successful in life. I was keen to listen to this because I knew that at times, someone else's failure is a warning and a lesson all at the same time that needed a heeding. As I wrote down my notes, his voice came back to me.

"The first of many reasons why people never become successful is their ego. A guru once told me that ego is an acrostic of 'edging God out.'"

 *"it's not just a book… it's medicine."*

I chuckled involuntarily when he said it but as I thought later about the explanation he gave, it made much more sense.

"'Ego' comes from the Latin word 'I.' When an individual is obsessed with himself, he will most likely ruin his own chances of success in life. This is because success requires humility, continuous learning and letting go of any preconceived ideas that you think you know about success. Such an individual may find it hard to embrace change."

"That sounds like pride to me," I said.

"Pride is in there for sure. One of the interesting things about pride is that you might not know you have it. It is so subtle to you but very pronounced to those who take some time to interact with you. It is still part of the ego."

"That's interesting, so how in the world do you tell someone is full of themselves as you have been interacting with people? What yardstick do you use?"

"Well, one doesn't need a yardstick. You will just recognize the ego when it rears its ugly face. But if you must have a list, you will easily identify the ego by the following. First, ego always wants to win an argument." He said clearly intent on proceeding to lay down his list.

I waved him to hold on for a while as I reflected because being a lawyer, I had to win all my arguments to be productive. Noticing the predicament, he chuckled. Not able to hold on to the laugh, he roared in a peal of teary laughter obviously remembering some jokes about lawyers.

"You must know that I am not talking about those kinds of arguments. I am talking about the insatiable sense to always be right on issues related to life. Well, you might be right but the attitude of not accommodating others' point of view even if wrong is a clear sign of a huge ego. A humble person will listen intently and be vulnerable enough to even consider that they could be wrong."

"Hmmm," I muttered.

"So, the next thing that can show you the existence of ego is always blaming other people when something doesn't go your way. It is like you do not want to take responsibility. This attitude will rob you of success since nobody wants to talk, work and engage with you if you are always blaming and complaining about other people."

I nodded in agreement.

"Third, ego will be exemplified by always beating yourself up whenever you fail at something. You set very high standards, almost to perfection and when you fail, it is a momentous occasion yet as we know failure will always be part of the journey to success, that's your ego talking."

"But don't we have to have high standards and be affected by our failures?"

"There is that and then there is seeing yourself as a failure. Failure is not a person. However, ego makes failure to be a person. When that happens, success becomes hard"

"Makes total sense."

"Fourth, you will know that there is a bout of ego when you don't listen to learn from others. This is perhaps the most obvious way to know the existence of ego."

"It is somehow connected to the first one, always wanting to win an argument." I offered.

"Yes. They are connected to the hip. If you did not want to listen to me, you would probably not learn a thing. A learning spirit doesn't differentiate a child from an elder. You know that you can learn from both at any given time. Ego will shut out the learning spirit because you are full of yourself, to begin with. The Nobody can tell you anything mentality. In the success equation, the more you learn and apply, the more you succeed." Therefore, you must teach yourself to be a good listener if you want to succeed.

"I couldn't agree more," I added.

"Perhaps the most sinister of all yardsticks of measuring the ego is this one: Never feeling good when someone else succeeds." Mr. Client left that hanging for a while then continued.

"No one is exempt from this one. We are all susceptible to feeling bad when our friends go ahead of us even as we are growing up. Part of that is because of the competitive society with which we grew up. However, as adults, we must put off those childish ways and learn to celebrate when others succeed. The more pained you are with someone else's success, the more the amount of ego exists in you. Ultimately, you will not succeed if this is the fuel for your success—to beat others to the game. There will always be someone better than you. There is great gain in contentment and we should learn it."

"Wait a minute," I interjected.

"You seem to me like a person who is not content. You keep increasing your wealth to date. I don't see you slowing down."

"That's a great observation. An outsider might think that all I am doing is increasing my wealth and yet all I am doing is growing and deploying all the potential that I can. But in all this, I am content in that I do not feel bad when someone else has more. It is not about how much one person has over the other. For me, it is growth and using opportunities available. I can't just sit and do nothing when I can grow. The agenda is not necessarily to get richer than my neighbor. The agenda is to be the best that I was created to be, and with that, I cannot be content until I achieve that potential". He said, emphasizing the word 'Cannot'.

"Very true," I was satisfied with his explanation.

"Lastly, you will know that there is an ego when you are a gossip. You keep talking about other people's flaws as you compare them with your perfect picture. You try people as the judge jury and executioner and always find them guilty. You then ruthlessly sentence them in your mind, speech and actions."

    *"it's not just a book… it's medicine."*

As I reflected and wrote down these points in my notebook, I was making a careful introspection about my life and ego. I could see some points in my life where the ego had reared its ugly head and yet I was unaware. I needed to be humble and accept to learn. Lawyers are normally called 'Learned Friends', but that doesn't mean that they know everything. I realized that I needed to come to terms with the fact that it was OK not to know, and it was OK to acknowledge and even tell people that I didn't know some things. That would open up the opportunity for more learning. I was satisfied even as I reflected when I remembered what Mr. Client had said that day.

"Everyone has an ego, and these are things that we have all been through. And the worst of them all is trying to deny the fact that you have an ego problem. Ego is bad for your success journey because it robs you of the opportunity to take risks. Life is all about risks. In fact, it has been said that the biggest risk is trying not to risk at all. An ego locks away your creative genius because you care too much about what others may say or think about you. People will always criticize and judge you, no matter what you do. They will judge you whether you are doing something or doing nothing at all. Get used to it. Realize that the people judging you are the ones with big egos, and you need not fall into their category." He said.

After a full reflection about the ego, I turned my attention to something else that Mr. Client had mentioned in passing but when I pressed him, he got really animated about it. So, in my notebook, I wrote at the top of the page: FEAR.

"I know it is cliché when we talk about fear, but perhaps I can tell you that nothing stands in the way of success so huge and imposing as fear does. Fear is a mystery because even though it is not physical, it has stopped the most eligible, most equipped and most prepared people on earth. To me, it is one of the most powerful enemies of success you can ever have. It doesn't discriminate. You can find as much fear at the presidential palace and military garrison as you can find on the streets."

"Tell me more about this, please. Have you had a first-time experience with it?"

"Perhaps I would be right to say that we all have fear in different ways and at different degrees. Perhaps I would also be right to say that the person who claims that they are not afraid might be the most fearful. But when it comes to being successful, most of us are hindered by fear than by our qualifications or lack thereof. That's why you find that the most successful of us are not necessarily the well-educated, but the most daring."

This was absolutely right as it referred to Mr. Client. He was not 'formally' educated as many people might think. I would say he was mostly self-educated.

"Fear weakens our immune system and can cause cardiovascular damage, gastrointestinal problems such as ulcers and irritable bowel syndrome, and decreased fertility. It leads to accelerated ageing and even premature death. That is concerning health. Each day, millions of individuals around the world write goals about how to live better lives, improve their health, have more meaningful relationships and make more money. They envision how their lives would be after they have achieved their goals; how great they would feel as couples and how happy their homes would be. But as time goes, this excitement fades away and becomes a distant dream on the horizon that they can never touch. Why? What happens to such individuals? Why do they give up so quickly and get back to their lives of quiet desperation? What paralyzes these once excited groups and prevents them from ever taking action?" He asked then answered promptly.

"One word: FEAR!" he laughed as we took a left turn. "Fear is the cage that keeps us from ever taking action, from letting go, from exploring the unknown and from taking risks. This sometimes is not our fault, to begin with. Growing up, we have always been taught to play safe and not stray too far. We have been conditioned to always live a life of 'fear.'" "Can you believe that in this era of globalization some people even fear to try out a dish from a different culture and eat the same kind of food from the time they are born till their old age?"

He went on and displayed a wealth of knowledge on the subject matter as if he was well acquainted with the fear itself:

"Fear will manifest in many ways or at least we succumb to fear in different dimensions. First, there is fear of pain.

Whether it is physical, emotional or whatever, we are generally afraid of pain to varying degrees depending on our experiences. But that fear of pain can keep you from succeeding because you will seldom find success there no being pain."

"I hear you."

"This is a constant reminder of the things that have not gone according to plan in the past. It is the disappointment we have suffered, the loneliness we have experienced, the lack we have endured, that forces us to cling onto what we have – physically and emotionally – out of a mindset and belief of scarcity. It is the assumption that if we let go of what we have, we may never get anything like it again. This is the fear that keeps people in jobs they don't like and in toxic relationships. All of us, when we were young, once or many times, were warned not to touch fire and not to live on the edge. Could some adults have become struck with these warnings, become risk-averse and failed to transition beyond these early childhood warnings?" He asked rhetorically.

"It is amazing that belief in scarcity is what cements the fear of pain!" I exclaimed.

"The ever wanting to maintain status quo is a veil that covers the fear of pain. Status quo is what has kept very many people at bay from success. To some extent, culture serves to insulate us from suffering pain. People would rather obey and worship their cultures than succeed. I know of a friend whose father could not buy land outside of his parents' blessings because no one in that family since Adam had done that. Unfortunately for him, his parents were also afraid and unexposed to such a transaction and thought that it would take their son away from the home. He eventually lost his job, never bought the land and was relegated to the country the rest of his life."

"Wow."

"Yes. Quite unfortunate. The other way fear manifests itself is through 'fear of now'. This arises from the belief that you are not qualified enough. You don't allow yourself to take the next step because you are afraid that you are not good enough or that you do not have enough resources. Some people have great ideas but cannot speak at meetings, other decline promotions while some decline nominations for elective office because of fear of not being qualified enough. The constant reminder by the little voice in your head keeps you dead in your tracks because you do not believe you have what it takes to move to the next level. As such, this self-doubt makes you think that you are undeserving of happiness, success or great wealth, and as long as that is your thought, you will not be successful. Even if one inherited great wealth and he or she has this kind of fear then this fear will make him or her lose it all!"

"Perfectly true!" I suffered from this ailment. I said.

"Thirdly, there is the fear of failure; this one is common to us all and perhaps the worst of all fears. It is the fear that we shall not get the results we desire because of one or more factors which we believe to be beyond our control. This is the fear that stops us from even trying out a new venture because we are afraid it may not succeed. It is also coupled with what people will think when we fail, and how painful it would be when we fail. You see, success probably has nothing to do with your capacity to succeed but everything to do with your capacity to conquer the fear of failure."

"That's interesting," I murmured out.

"Yes. A less educated person that is daring has a greater chance than a well-educated person that is timid. Teddy Roosevelt has a powerful quote that is hanging in the walls of my children's rooms: *'Far much better it is to dare mighty things, to win glorious triumphs even though checkered by failure than to take rank with those poor spirits who neither enjoy nor suffer much because they live in a great twilight that neither knows victory nor defeat.'*"

I felt goosebumps all over my body when Mr. Client quoted it with so much passion and without hesitation. Not only was it articulate, but it was also absolutely inspiring.

"The kids must be breaking stuff at home since they have no fear," I chuckled.

"Well, you could say that. Allowing them to dare even at my own expense is one powerful way of teaching them to learn. However, I also teach them to own the failure but never to fail to dare."

"Oh." I listened in awe.

"My friend, I am sure you might have seen books and volumes upon volumes written about fear. I could go on and on about it, but I would like you to know that it is a monster. A bad one at that. The fourth fear is the fear of the unknown, and we all have this. Some people have a very unreasonable fear of venturing into anything that they feel is beyond their knowledge and control. They would like to stay doing what they were taught in school or only those things that they are very familiar with. They also spend a lifetime planning but never taking action. They are skeptical about simple truths. For example, they can never believe that it's through giving that we receive. We gather evidence of how other people have failed and use it to discourage ourselves from ever giving anything a try.

Knowing what fears are holding you prisoner is instrumental in helping you break free from its claws. Also, speak to successful people or seek professional help if fear is a hindrance to your pursuit of a successful life." He explained and then kept quiet. It was the end of his impromptu teaching on the subject of fear.

I wrote in my notebook as I reflected and continued to do introspection. I saw exactly where my fears lay. I was traditional and old-schooled even though I thought I was modern and in 'vogue'. I realized that I was afraid of anything outside of my Law practice. To succeed in life and attain the dream that I wanted, I had to deal with that fear and dismantle the structures that I had created. I remembered reading Robin Sharma's book, *The Monk Who Sold His Ferrari.* The book talked about a lawyer who tried to make it successful in life and nearly crashed his health in the process. I knew that I had to deal with the fear of now, fear of the unknown and break my hold of the status quo.

I breathed out heavily, put my notebook down and paced my room a little, letting Mr. Client's words about fear bombard my psyche and do their work in changing me. Walking to the fridge, I picked up some cold juice and continued my meditation. It was one of the rare things I did—working on myself and for some reason, today seemed like I had all the strength and motivation to do it. I knew there was so much to reflect upon and act on too. That's why I also put my timetable next to me. It had been changed and updated several times with each meeting from Mr. Client.

I knew that I had to restructure it once more as things were taking shape. After a good moment of thinking about my life and how it has been affected by fear, I determined to take action appropriately. I went back to my notebook and quickly wanted to capture the next thing that had intrigued me as Mr. Client drove me towards home. Someone had crossed the road where there was no demarcation for pedestrian crossing. As they did so, they were so nonchalant about it as if it wasn't up to them to be safe. Mr. Client had obviously been used to such scenarios, but he saw an opportunity to draw a lesson out of it.

"Did you see that?" He asked.

 

"Yeah," I did.

"It's like he hates his life."

"It's just being complacent about his safety and life in general. What if the car's brakes are not working? I mean, how sure is he that I wouldn't hit him and toss him out of the road?"

I imagined the 'toss' then laughed out hysterically.

Mr. Client smiled at his dry humor but then instantly got serious.

"I see the same thing in business nearly every day. People are just plain old complacent."

"Oh really?" I got more interested and when Mr. Client saw that I was alert, he figuratively put on a teacher's cap.

"Another reason people are not successful in life is complacency." He said. "According to Dictionary.com, complacent means "pleased, especially with oneself or one's merits, advantages, situation, etc., often without awareness of some potential danger or defect; self-satisfied."

"Hold on. You are a walking dictionary now?"

He roared in laughter, wiped his eyes then explained.

"I literally studied that word for a season of time, I kid you not. It was creeping into my business, my personal life and my family. We actually lost a huge deal one time at the company because we were complacent. I was complacent.

Complacency even in a matter of margins can cost you your life just like that man unenthusiastically crossing the road a few moments back."

I tried to imagine Mr. Client in such a complacent situation.

"I saw it again: One of the top enemies of success is complacency. A kind of feeling which makes individuals unwilling to take any steps because they feel like they are already okay where they are. Well, they may be okay in their own estimates, but many times it is just an illusion and an excuse to avoid taking greater actions. I have realized that without constant review, you will easily fall into complacency thinking that you are OK. I am sure you can mention some major companies that were complacent and for that reason alone, they are non-existent." He added. I nodded thinking of Nokia, a company that was the leading cell phone manufacturer in the world with tens of millions of handsets sold in under five years. When smartphones came, Nokia, in my opinion, was complacent and now they are no more. I also thought of Motorola that used to push Nokia in the same niche. I thought of Kodak who invented digital photography decades before smartphones came but never rolled it out. I told Mr. Client about these companies and he agreed, shaking his head as if those losses were personal and pained him."

"I came up with a five-point plan to curb complacency."

"Hold on one minute." I requested him as I took out my smartphone, put on the audio recorder and let him loose.

 

I should have been smarter to know that this man was a walking success, motivation and inspiration house. Quite a lot that he had said had been lessons that could be lost unless someone was alert. He smiled knowingly and apologized for not telling me that the lesson was on. His reason was that he wasn't really teaching as he would have. Nevertheless, I thought that it was important to note.

"First, Find pain points. If you feel like you are being complacent, it is highly likely that you are in your comfort zone. When we are in our comfort zone, we are very much less likely to want to change the situation. Realize that much as things seem "okay" they can be better. Secondly, look around your life or situation, and try to identify the pain points. Ask yourself, what don't I like about my life? That's a sure way of finding out if you are complacent."

I nodded as I looked over my recorder to ascertain that it was recording.

"Secondly, find a vision. Once you realize that things can actually become better than they already are, you set the stage for creating a picture of a better future. Now is the time to dream. Let your mind wander, think about how your life would be if you did not have to worry about money or anything else in life. Where would you be living? Which cars would you be driving? What kind of family would you be having? How would you spend your weekends? How would you be feeling?"

He looked at me to signal that his point was already made then went on.

"Third, set goals. We have mentioned before that nothing worthwhile is achieved without proper goals and deliberate planning. Write down your goals and create action steps for their realization. A goal with a deadline, written together with clearly defined action steps and a daily task list is the best way to knock you out of complacency. Start implementing your plan immediately. What can you do today, to help you plan and achieve the future you desire?" He concluded.

As I remembered that, I took my notebook and switched on my recorder to just take in the teaching from Mr. Client. He was hitting the nail right on the head. I saw how complacent I was in many areas of my life. I was complacent with my health, my career, my relationships and my personal growth. Clearly, there was so much to work on in my life. After figuring out the changes that I needed to make in my life, I hit the 'play' button and listened even more.

"Complacency is a killer of success; unlike anything, I have seen. But there is one more thing that you should be aware of that I just realized as that man crossed the road. If I was not focused, he would be dead by now. If I was not alert, it would have been fatal. Therefore, one of the things that kill success, a great enemy of success is either lack of focus or broken focus."

"Aha?"

 *"it's not just a book… it's medicine."*

"You have a brilliant project. You have started working on it. It is promising. You are excited. The future looks bright. Then you hit an obstacle. You get frustrated. Another business idea pops up in your mind. You abandon the first project. You start working on the new idea. You are excited. The future looks bright… Familiar? You are suffering from a lack of focus. Lots of activities with no productivity. Ten years after, you have not achieved anything simply because you are always on gear one: the starting point.

FOCUS is what will help you stay the course even when the tides seem to be going against you. It will help you increase your performance, lead to increased and faster results and ultimately propel you towards your dream of financial freedom. Failure to focus is like shooting a gun in a dark room. Good luck hitting a target. What you need to do is to turn on the lights, find your target, then shoot. Focus is not only about finding the target; it is also about sticking to your target. F.O.C.U.S has many times been described as Following One Course Until Successful." He explained.

As we came close to my home, Mr. Client parked his car near a shopping mall. He was intent on getting something on the way back home. I knew that I needed to glean so much from him because for the most part, he was building on the lessons he had shared earlier on in the day about the protection of wealth, but he was as well sharing about the enemies of success.

"So far, I have learnt from you in passing that there are different enemies of success. You have talked about lack of focus, the ego, fear and so on, but could there be other things that can hinder my success that I need to be aware of?

Mr. Client switched on the engine, then matter-of-factly started teaching as he counted with his fingers.

"The enemy of letting lack of capital hold you back is another great one that you must watch out for."

I was all ears since this was relevant to me.

"I have come across countless people with solid business ideas, but which will never be executed for one simple factor: Capital. They believe that they can never get their businesses off the ground if they don't have solid funding behind them. You have probably heard about the startups that soared because of the funding they received, but I bet you haven't heard about those that failed miserably despite the huge capital injections they received. If your business idea isn't solid enough, no amount of capital can save you from failure. Do you have a great idea but little or no money for a startup? Don't let that stop you! There certainly will be days when you will be stressed, but that is what entrepreneurship is all about: Making things happen despite the challenges. There are numerous articles and books about how you can start and run a business with minimal capital. My personal favorite book is, *'How To Start A Business With No Money'* by Rachael Bridge. Some ideas

 *"it's not just a book… it's medicine."*

include building a business around your expertise so that you can eliminate the costly consultants, taking advantage of free marketing and advertising and telling everyone about the business you are doing." He explained. I nodded.

"Of course, another enemy of success is the usual money myths. These are misconceptions about money, wealth and success. Everyone has their own opinions about money, wealth and success, and they are probably right according to their experiences, interests and goals. Many people hear about these myths from parents and relatives, or from poor and unsuccessful people when growing up. The myths then stick with them throughout their lives. Money myths are dangerous because they promote a negative attitude about wealth which discourages people from becoming financially free."

Mr. Client seemed to have remembered something. He looked through the glove compartment of his car and found a pen drive titled "Money Myths."

"This is less than ten minutes and since you are recording, I need you to hear this." He cranked up the volume of the stereo as a crisp sound of a leading personal financial guru broke through the system and read out the title: "Money Myths."

Some of the common money myths include:

**Money is the source of all evil;** This myth has been said time and time again. It is important to note that it is quoted wrongly from the Bible. The Bible does not say, Money is the source of all evil. It says the love of money is the root cause of all evil. Many people look at money as a necessary evil, but it is not. The (excessive) love for money where some people will do anything to get it is what is condemned. As seen in the earlier chapters, the best way to get rich is through employing your creative processes namely finding a problem in society and solving it. Money can be a powerful source of good. For example, Bill and Melinda Gates through their foundation have donated millions of dollars to charities around the world to provide clean water, food and health services to the poor. You can become wealthy and use your money to positively impact the lives of people around you and those you may never meet. Used properly, money is not a source of evil but a powerful source for good causes.

**A higher-income will make you wealthy;** This may be true for some people, but for others, a higher income does not automatically translate into a higher net worth. More often than not, a higher income comes along with higher expenses. As our monies grow, so do our wants. It takes an advanced level of discipline to avoid spending unnecessarily.

I am not saying that it is bad to enjoy some of your income. Nothing wrong with that. All I am saying is that a higher income does not automatically translate into a better net worth. It takes budgeting, paying attention to spending and focusing on long term financial goals to achieve financial freedom.

 *"it's not just a book… it's medicine."*

**Only brilliant and talented people can become rich;** All persons are capable of becoming rich when they follow the basic truths in this book. Educated people can be rich and so can illiterates, those who live in the city and those in the countryside, talented people and outstanding people can be rich and so can average people. You have the primary tools to become rich, you simply have to sharpen them and put them to the best possible use.

**Debt is bad;** This is another common misconception that some people – people who struggle most of their lives – fail to grasp. They try to avoid debt altogether. By now you know that there is good debt and bad debt: good debt is debt that someone else pays on your behalf whereas bad debt is debt that you personally have to pay. You should avoid bad debt at all costs but embrace good debt as much as you can. You have probably heard of the phrase "Other People's Money" (OPM) – that is how the rich get rich: by using other people's money to build investments that pay them a steady cash flow.

That having been said, I also caution you from carelessly and overly diving into borrowing as it can be disastrous. Rather, take calculated steps according to your investment plan.

Well used debt – good debt – is your first-class ticket to financial freedom.

**You need to have a lot of money before you can start saving and investing;** Many of us are struggling with bills and expenses and are not saving enough money at the end of the month. Because we are not making much progress, we easily get discouraged because we do not see any substantial increases in our savings accounts. For example, someone saving 1% on their income can easily get discouraged and decide against saving altogether simply because the money seems too small to make any substantial investment move.

What these people don't know is that there is a power called compounding. As small as your monthly saving is, over the years, your investment can be massive because of the snowball effect.

You do not have to wait till you are earning a higher income or till you pay off your debt to start saving and investing. The few dollars added each month can actually pay off your debt and help you become financially free in a much shorter time. So, take action now, start saving and plan your next investment immediately.

**Good opportunities have already been taken or monopolized;** This myth is commonly found among the lazy and excuse-oriented people. They find a reason for their inaction and blame other people for their situation. They mistakenly believe that opportunities have been taken or monopolized by others. The truth is that there are a thousand opportunities for every individual on earth.

The opportunities to serve others and be paid are truly inexhaustible. Thousands of opportunities are created every day by technology. New professions, that the last generation never dreamt of, are created on a daily basis around the world. Look closely and you will see thousands of opportunities around you.

**Big companies and cartels will never allow the poor and middle classes to succeed;** The myth that some people have planned to make you destitute is simply self-destruction. It is also giving other people too much power over yourself.

In general, big companies will be too happy to buy your good idea or product. They are always on the lookout for hardworking, trustworthy and innovative people to work with.

Some companies will be willing to support and even partner with start-ups and young entrepreneurs.

**Insurance is for the rich;** Many people still perceive insurance to be for the rich. They consider it a luxury, an investment reserved only for the few well-off individuals. Low-income individuals have felt that they cannot afford premiums because they lack regular jobs or simply because they aren't making enough money. Some are too busy creating wealth that they forget to protect it.

As we have already seen, insurance affords you asset and wealth protection so that you do not lose your fortune due to unavoidable circumstances.

Life insurance, on the other hand, allows you to financially secure your future, alongside your family's well-being in case anything happens to you and you are not able to provide for them. This means that life insurance is for all categories of people, regardless of one's financial position." He concluded.

Mr. Client switched the stereo off and looked at me. I was nodding and agreeing with all that I had heard. Of course, he had already mentioned some of those things in our lessons. I didn't know how to thank him. I felt very indebted to him and knew that one of the ways I could pay my teacher was to become successful myself. We spent another thirty minutes or so in the car as he explained about other things that he felt were important and couldn't be left unsaid. Thereafter, we had said our goodbyes with a confirmation of our date the following day at his residence.

So, as I looked over my notebook and timetable, things were taking shape. I was shocked at how time had flown. Normally, I would watch the news but that evening, it didn't feel any important anymore. I had spent a significate amount of time watching and listening to news, this had not taught me much except for the helplessness and tragedies in distant lands. I now had more valuable things in my life to sort out. There was still much to reflect about our meeting and I still had quite some notes to take and some plans to make. Knowing that I needed to leverage on the "flow" that I was experiencing at the moment without tiring myself, I rested a little once again. I took walks in the house as

 *"it's not just a book… it's medicine."*

I thought and reflected. Nobody would have told me that I would be in this wonderful, stretched situation a few days back. It is amazing how a single week can change the outlook of your life if you immerse yourself in gathering potent and actionable information that comes from a source that embodies it! I couldn't believe my luck or blessing in meeting Mr. Client. Although it was embarrassing asking him for a quick loan, it turned out well after all. Indeed, it is true that questions in life are answers.

## Practical Guide To Your Millions

1. Kill your ego and know when it becomes an obstacle to your goals and quest for financial freedom.

2. Take action in spite of fear.

3. Ignore the money myths. These are tightly held onto by the poor and unsuccessful. The only lesson you can learn from them is to avoid the mistakes they made. Their lives serve as a living warning to you.

4. Look past your lack of capital and find a way through implementing your ideas.

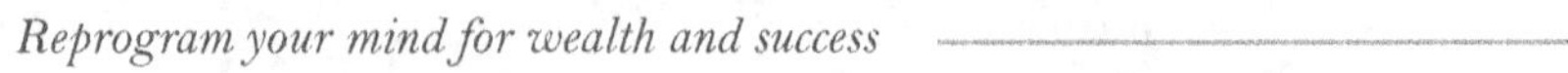

**CHAPTER**

# GUARDING & NOURISHING YOUR THOUGHTS

*"Just as a monkey swinging through the trees grabs one branch and lets it go to seize another, so too, that which is called thought, mind or consciousness arises and disappears continually both day and night."- Gautama Buddha.*

In all of Mr. Client's properties, there was an imposing theme of nature, vegetation and the environment. He loved water and plants, flowers and grass. I got to notice that and I asked him what the inspiration behind it was. He mentioned that he learnt that from the near obsession that one of his uncles that he admired had. In one of the properties, a professional gardener was tending the flowers and trimming the hedges, watering and fertilizing others. Mr. Client seemed impressed and satisfied with what the gardener was doing. He engaged in small talk with him as if they were long lost friends before we resumed our tour.

It is at that moment, I recalled that Mr. Client launched into another important admonition that I knew emanated from the things he loved to do.

"Do you know that our minds and thoughts need to be protected and nourished the same way he is tending to the greenery? Did you know that the same applies to our physical bodies?" He asked.

"Well, you could say that it is common knowledge, especially about the physical body"

"Wealthy people who are enjoying their wealth do apply a high level of nourishing routines in their lifestyles. They watch their health like a hawk. They watch their thoughts and minds like it is a treasure."

I nodded as I showed him that I wanted to hear more.

"I want to teach you about controlling your thoughts." Mr. Client offered. I became more attentive.

"Thoughts, although invisible at first, are living things and are energy that lives forever. Thoughts become words that translate into actions then into habits and if left unguarded may result in addictions. Thoughts are so powerful that some people have proclaimed that we are literarily what we think about.

Thousands of years ago, Buddha described the human mind as being filled with drunken monkeys, jumping around, screeching, chattering, carrying on endlessly."

We both chuckled telepathically. We had become accustomed to each other's light humor and of late we had started complimenting each other as we made light moments of situations.

"Scientists estimate that the human mind has over seventy thousand different thoughts in a single day, the majority of which will be negative."

"Wow. And that's just natural and automatic?"

"Yes, unfortunately. And that's why the secret is in nourishing your thoughts actively, consistently and intentionally. Otherwise, we naturally are at the mercy of our negative thoughts. They paint our world in a negative illusion. You will be shocked that most of the negative things we believe about ourselves and our future are illusions. However, once an illusion has been believed long enough, it becomes reality."

"Wow!"

"Negative thoughts are known to cause paranoia, irrational fears, anxiety, depression and illness. Some people I know have died more from negative thoughts, irrational fears and effects of societal stigma than from the diseases they suffered from. Negative thoughts of self-doubt when not decisively dealt with will delay or even lay to waste dreams of financial freedom.

Uncontrolled thoughts can also lead to analysis paralysis which hampers our ability to take action on our goals and dreams. This explains why some people seem stuck in the same position - unable to move the proverbial needle."

This made total sense to me as I reflected. I began to see even as I was jotting down my action points in my notebook that evening how I had been subtly affected by my negative thoughts. At some point in time, friends had complained that I was too negative and pessimistic. I didn't realize I was until they said it. Now that Mr. Client was raising the same issue that day, it all came back to me.

"The media, advertisers, Hollywood and influencers fuel our minds with different fears, hopes, violence and threats. The majority of us consume this information without any filters. A person who masters his or her thought process, throwing out and avoiding sources of negative thoughts will attain anything they desire. They will attain peace when there is turmoil around them or wealth when surrounded by poverty."

"I hear you," I said.

"Mind control is a thing actually. It is an ever-present thing today. The question is: Who will control your mind? Is it someone else or is it you? Wealthy people will never have their minds controlled by someone else. They will do it themselves."

I had nodded and then asked. "How exactly do they achieve that? How can they really control their minds? I thought it

 *"it's not just a book… it's medicine."*

was not an easy thing because the mind has a mind of its own."

"That's why nourishing is an intentional thing. Let me ask you. What do you notice about my office when you come visiting? What really stands out for you?"

I thought for a minute then replied.

"I think you are meticulous about its appearance."

"So, what exactly stands out for you?"

"I must admit I thought it weird to have quotes all over the place and framed in an expensive way." I quipped.

"That is a deliberate part of nourishing my thoughts. To surround yourself with thought leaders such as Elon Musk as you saw in my office it to somehow tune into their thought's wavelength. You see, if you just leave your environment like that is to let it on autopilot which by default drifts towards negativity."

"Wow." I had exclaimed.

I took some time to look around my apartment. There was nothing particularly nourishing about it and my thoughts at that moment. I had to act. I recalled again what Mr. Client had said about controlling the mind.

"As I said earlier, mind control is about intentionality. First, you have to understand that your thoughts are not always real. For instance, thoughts about what other people think about you may turn out to be completely untrue and irrational. Negative thoughts about yourself resulting from what other people think or say, however close to you they are, may not be true and must be rebuffed and rebuked. Some people who have failed to achieve their goals or even have no goals, feel inadequate, are envious and have no purpose. Do not allow their mean words or false prophesies to affect your destiny. Woe to you if your life is dictated by what you think other people think or even should think about you."

I had smiled at the way Mr. Client was adept with his analogies and language. He noticed my smile and pretended to be serious then continued.

"Second, you have to replace disempowering thoughts and questions with empowering ones. Remember the quote about wild monkeys in our heads? It's true. The worst you can do is to silently accede to the negative and disempowering thoughts. For what you tolerate, you will eventually accept and it will rule your life. If you think you are stupid, I cannot help you until that thought is uprooted. If you think you are not good enough, to succeed, you must confront that thought incessantly and replace it with another empowering one such as, I know that I have the full capacity to succeed. In fact, it would even be better to let your mind look for answers by posing a question such as: what can I do to succeed? In so doing subconsciously you have already accepted that you will succeed and all that is needed is to find a way."

As I thought about it, I had to pause and marvel at how easy it had been for me to accept and accede to negative thoughts in my life almost all my adult life. It was a silent epidemic. There were very many thoughts that I had to confront head-on. People saw me as a high-flying attorney but actually inside of me, I never imagined that I could be successful all round in life. That thought had to be dealt with. I took note of it and continued reflecting on what Mr. Client was teaching me about nourishing my thoughts intentionally.

"As you already know, thoughts do not just come from out of the blue. For the most part, always remember that your thoughts are influenced by your environment, information from the media, friends, parents or teachers. Change these to a more positive environment and consume more useful and helpful information."

I realized that every source of information has an agenda, and for the most part, that agenda doesn't primarily benefit me. I thought about how I consumed news, magazines, gossip, politics, sports and all. My environment was actually littered with all these things because I wasn't intent on controlling my thoughts and nourishing them. Something had to be done in that department, I noted.

"Once you have cleared your environment of the dangerous and undesirable thought weeds, you now start watering your mind and nourishing it with a good source of positive, instructive, motivational and inspirational thought doses.

These are just the right seeds that the mind can flourish on. So, look at how you can redirect your thoughts by giving heed to positive stimuli for your thoughts."

"Makes total sense," I said.

"You also need to have a high sense of Self-awareness: understand what causes you to have negative thoughts and when the thoughts occur. Study the trends and become aware of them. Also, continue to find time to meditate and pray so that you can deliberately nourish your thoughts positively"

Remembering the gardener, Mr. Client said "our minds and thoughts are like gardens and we are the gardeners. If we take good care of our gardens, we get beautiful flowers or a bumper harvest but when we neglect the garden, it gets attacked by weeds and pests. The weeds and pests are negative thoughts and negative habits. Take care of your thoughts and your thoughts will take care of you." He advised. "So, I can see it's a two-pronged approach. You not only have to be defensive and watch what comes in, but you also have to be proactive and be in charge of what comes in," I said.

"That's right. I can never over-emphasize the need for nourishing your mind if you have to be successful. It seems as if people are only interested in the 'secrets' and the 'How Tos' that I have already shared with you. However, the mind is the engine surrounding the hive of activity that will lead you to your wealth. So, guard it. Guard your heart. Guard your mind. Be diligent while at it. Feed it royally. I will just give you a few pointers on nourishing your mind and I am sure you already know this."

I had nodded and signaled that I was ready to receive what he had to say.

"First, read books that teach you self-improvement and those that help you achieve your goals. If you want to be wealthy and successful, read relevant books. Watching horror movies will be counterproductive and will induce thoughts of fear."

I had felt satisfied that I was already doing this. Atomic Habits was my latest read and I was enjoying it immensely.

"Second, carefully choose the content of what you watch and listen to. These should reflect your values and aspirations. Third, practice mindfulness; be mindful of your speech and actions."

"I keep hearing about mindfulness a lot these days. It almost sounded like it was an Eastern Mystic religion or something." I had shot back.

"Well, don't be so quick to label things. Mindfulness is a deep practice of being in the moment. The disciplined have learnt to be at peace in their mind even when there is a fracas all around them. It is a practice. Not a gift. The more you practice mindfulness, the more adept you are. The more you are mindful, the more you are able to channel your thoughts properly and make great decisions.

"Remember to also seek the company of people who are successful in the fields of your interest. Be in their presence. Listen to their language. Hear them talk about billions of dollars worth of projects and contracts even if you have no money in your pocket. You are nourishing your mind royally. Don't be comfortable in the presence of those that marvel at your greatness. Be comfortable in the company of those that make you feel tiny, unqualified, and needing to grow."

"Wow."

"Yes. Perhaps it is one of the most powerful shortcuts for growth. Hanging around incredible people rubs off of you. It starts affecting your mind. However, even in that state, remember to practice gratitude. A positive mind looks for all the things that it can be grateful for because, to be honest with you, people do not need motivation to be ungrateful. Negativity is all around us and it is sold as news. So, learn to be grateful every day. That spirit of gratitude pollinates your mind to look for more positive things. It empowers you to see the world as a good place not a place of suffering. If your thought pattern tells you that you are a sufferer, that's exactly what you will attract. You are not a victim. A spirit of gratitude will help you more than you will ever know." He had explained.

"Finally," he said, "If I can think of anything that will help you to nourish your mind, I would tell you to be focused and single-minded. Doing too many things at a go will sidetrack you as it is counterproductive. So, plan your life out as often as possible to the dregs of details. Spend as much time as you can to plan your day before it begins. Perhaps also just plan your week ahead of time. Great and successful people know how important it is to have their whole month planned out. It helps them to focus and thus nourish their minds."

"One more thing…" I smiled for I knew that he was so full of information that he could never really say 'finally' successfully. Looking at me, he smiled too and continued. "Practice positive self-talk. People call it affirmations. Others call them incantations. As long as they are powerful, addressing the self, positive and in the present tense, the words you speak to yourself out loud are like a nuclear bomb that dismisses all the negativity around your mind. You will have to say these words over and over and over again at an instance taking at least five minutes to repeat an incantation."

"Do you have one I can borrow?" I quickly asked not expecting him to tell me.

"I could give you mine, but it won't help you. It speaks to my state in its context. Someone could say something like 'Every day in every way I am getting better and better, yes!' They could repeat that incantation for minutes until they are charged up if you know what I mean. This is much more powerful than being quiet and accepting the dull or negative thoughts swirling around your mind."

"It makes perfect sense", I said and Mr. Client had stopped talking about nourishing the mind.

As I reflected, I knew that my work had been cut out. There were a lot of changes that needed to be done in my life. My notebook was full. My timetable needed an overhaul. It was like someone had laid my mind to waste and it was a fully-fledged construction site of sorts. I glanced at my watch; it was 11:47 pm. This was a first. Staying up that late to just focus on me. I must say, I was very happy for this so much so that I did not realize how exhausted I was. Taking a quick hot shower, I retired to bed a man on a personal mission to change himself and achieve his full potential.

## Practical Guide To Your Millions

1. Guard your mind militantly from negative thoughts and sources of negative information.

2. Deliberately nourish positive thoughts by reading positive, instructive, motivational and inspirational books or other such informational material.

3. Control your mind no one should do it for you.

4. Practice positive self-talk and view yourself favorably with a capacity to succeed and attain your financial goals.

 *"it's not just a book… it's medicine."*

**CHAPTER**

# THE GOLDEN HABITS OF SUCCESS

*"We are what we repeatedly do. Excellence, then, is not an act, but a habit."* – **Will Durant.**

## Sunday

Time seemed to have stopped. I thought. "In fact, Sundays are really slow days," I said to myself. Time check: 3:30 pm. This whole day, I had been anxiously waiting for 6:00 pm but it wasn't reaching. "I will go early," I said to myself. I picked the piece of paper that had his address, started my car and drove off to look for his home. I will be like him one day, I thought. Then I laughed at myself. This one week had been the best week of my life. I had never felt in charge like this before.

It took me about one hour to get to his neighborhood. I had never been to that side of town. What a rich neighborhood! - quiet, exquisite, and classy. Finding his house was not difficult – Google maps and GPS were handy. I paused outside the gate for a while, admiring the exterior. The fence was long and high. The wall was lined with trees of different kinds and flowers. The exterior looked like a florist's nursery.

The neighborhood was well organized with almost similar houses, all overlooking one of the largest freshwater lakes in the world. The air was fresh and friendly. What a sharp contrast to the slums and other areas where the poor - and middle-class families lived!

The gatekeeper should have seen me through the CCTV because he came out of the side gate without me hooting or touching the bell. He greeted me politely and asked for my name.

I told him who I was.

"Oh! We have been expecting you. Please come in." His face lit up as he spoke. He tapped a button on the remote controller and the gate slid open letting me in.

As I drove through the driveway, I didn't know what to focus on: the house, the cars parked or the children playing in the compound.

The house was big; three floors. It had an exotic 19th-century European touch. There seemed to be plants everywhere. The house was surrounded by a large compound with carefully trimmed and well-maintained gardens. To the left, was what looked like an amusement park. It had a bouncing castle, swings, unicorns and many other child play items. I could not see beyond the play area but there seemed to be a lot more space behind the house. His house had the best view of the lake in all the neighborhood.

I parked and got out of the car. Mr. Client together with his wife were waiting for me. I had met her only once or twice before but from the smile on her face, I could tell that husband must have told her about me and our lessons.

"Look who's early for dinner!" He exclaimed. I laughed shyly.

They welcomed me to their home and we went inside the living room. I was greeted by the most beautiful chandeliers. His wife, Rose, offered me a seat. Immediately, I was served a glass of cold fresh juice. They always have juice ready for guests, I thought. The living room was large, with big white leather chairs. These must be from the middle east, I thought to myself. Everything was perfect. The mini library, the dining, the neatness. This is a five-star home. I said to myself.

"This is a beautiful home you got," I told the couple as my eyes moved around like a roaming camera capturing a movie scene.

"Thank you. We have built it over time. Someday you will have a place like this." He said.

"Someday," I repeated. This is what it means to be rich. This is the life I deserve. I told myself.

Then his children came in to greet me. Cynthia, the eldest was the first. She should be about sixteen. Then came Damian, about two years younger and Lythia who was about ten, came following.

We did small talk about everything else apart from work. To Mr. Client, home was a no-work zone. They didn't even have a home office. His wife asked me several questions though.

She asked about where I lived, my family and my work. She would urge me to speak whenever she noticed I felt uncomfortable. And she never assumed anything. She always made sure the answer was mine. She made me promise not to use the phrase "You know" while answering her questions. Mr. Client just smiled and laughed, occasionally chipping in a word or two in my support. He was like a spectator in a tennis match with his wife Rose asking questions and me answering. She listened attentively to each word that came out of my mouth. Rose was the easiest person to talk to – the second being Mr. Client. It felt like a trip to a therapist.

I shared so much about myself that evening in that short time that I hardly realize it was 6:00 pm.

 

Jumping to his feet, Mr. Client asked his wife if he could "borrow" me for a moment.

"Sure." She said, "Dinner is ready."

"Great!" He exclaimed. "We'll be right with you after our brief tour."

So, he went ahead to show me around his home. He had a gym, sauna and steam bath in a separate house, much smaller than the main one. He did not have a garage, so all their cars were parked in the compound, each under its own tent. I quickly counted five expensive cars – a sedan, two SUVs, a pick-up truck and a family van.

Then we got to the other side of the house. The compound was even much larger than I had imagined. A garden on the left, a swimming pool in the middle and the children's play area on the other side and what looked like a minibar at the extreme end.

The compound was strikingly beautiful, with different species of plants. There were lights at every point in the gardens. This must be their favorite part of the home, I thought. Since the sun was setting, the place looked like one of those beautiful homes you see in a real estate magazine. There were bulbs at almost every point, although the solar lights had not yet been switched on. I wondered how the place looked after sunset with all those lights turned on.

"This is my wife's favorite part of the home. She spends most of her time here." Mr. Client remarked.

Dinner was set in the gardens. Everyone quickly arrived and so began the most amazing dinner I had ever had.

The children told me about themselves, their schools, what they love doing, how they help each other, how their parents are the best in the world. They asked if I had kids… They asked a lot of questions and dug for detailed answers. They were very curious to learn new ideas. I knew where they got that trait from.

Midway through the dinner, Mr. Client said to everyone, "And now, our favorite part of the dinner."

"Yesss!!!" The children shouted.

"And what was the assignment?" He asked.

"The golden habits of success." They shouted again in unison. "Yessss!" He exclaimed, looking more excited than ever. "And who's giving us our first point?" He asked.

All the kids had their hands up. He picked the youngest, Lythia.

"Praying daily." She started… "Prayer opens doors in all areas of our lives and keeps us strong when we feel overwhelmed. Prayer is how we communicate and make requests for God to answer." She concluded.

"Yess! Well done." Mr. Client said as everyone clapped and cheered Lythia on.

 

"Prayer is an avenue to resolution, the path to finding an answer to a problem. Prayer is the master key. It is written, "So I say to you: Ask and it will be given to you; seek and you will find; knock and the door will be opened to you. For everyone who asks receives; the one who seeks finds; and to the one who knocks, the door will be opened." "Pray with absolute faith that your petitions will be granted" Thousands of successful people across cultures and over the ages have set aside time to pray and meditate- mostly in the mornings. Some religions encourage their followers to pray several times a day at regular intervals. Sincere prayer and meditation are worthy habits. Mr. Client explained further.

I was getting challenged already.

"Next?" Mr. Client called out. Again, hands were up. He picked Cynthia.

**"Setting aside time for family and friends."** She began. Family time offers many benefits, including building confidence, creating a strong bond between family members and friends, improving communication skills, better performance in school and providing an opportunity to make memories built on fun, laughter, love and togetherness." Cynthia spoke with such confidence as one who is giving a lecture on the most familiar topics. She was such a confident and effective communicator - much better than many adults who could not clearly express themselves.

Everyone clapped for her. Everyone was excited.

Cheering and clapping continued. The dinner felt like an episode of America's Got Talent, with everyone shouting and cheering every time participants got on stage and gave a heartfelt performance. I wondered what it felt like to spend such a time with my family. Now I know why it is impossible to get Mr. Client on Sunday evenings. The experience was priceless. The children were self-disciplined, curious and eager to learn.

**"Offering more value."** Cynthia, the eldest child gave her second point. The key to success is to always do more than what you are paid for and that is where growth starts because now you have to learn how to be effective and efficient. When you have a reputation of doing more than what you have been asked to do, people notice it and that is how you get the best grades in class. That is also how you get promoted at work."

"And how do you go about that?" Mr. Client asked his sixteen-or-so-year-old daughter.

"Easy. She replied. "You just have to assume you have two jobs and you have only half the time you have been given to accomplish your tasks. Then you have to work faster. You will eventually have more time to help others out. Secondly, make friends with smart, respectful and successful people, learn new skills and then you can always ask for more responsibilities. I do that all the time at school. I always ask for more homework, but I still get time to help Damian and Lythia."

 

Again, everyone clapped and cheered.

I was getting beaten by these young champions. They knew more about habits than most adults. As a child, the only habit I had learnt at the dinner table was, "do not talk while eating." The rich surely do things differently, I agreed.

I was impressed by how the children seemed to have already mastered the habits that are needed to succeed in life. Mr. Client had taught his family well. I complimented him and his wife for teaching their children how to succeed at such an early age. These children were better prepared to serve their community than many adults I knew.

What a dinner I was having! I had never met a group of young stars this focused and intelligent. They seemed to be in some sort of competition to impress their parents. Their mother was the happiest. She laughed and clapped the loudest. The children seemed to copy her. They were one happy family.

Mr. Client genuinely accepted my compliments and added a few more habits.

## Controlling your emotions

"Emotions determine how you interact with people – both at school and at work, how you answer questions, how you spend the money in your piggie bank, what you do and how you deal with challenges and opportunities. Managing your emotions is not the same as suppressing them – which only leads to unwanted behaviors like watching TV too much, eating too much food and many others." He said drawing everyone's laughter. Lythia laughed loudest.

"When you are in a bad mood, he continued, avoid engaging in activities that will keep your mood bad – like watching sad movies or isolating yourself. What you have to do is engage in mood boosters. Talk to a friend with similar aspirations about something awesome, go for a walk, listen to uplifting music or better still read an inspiring book. I love to visit my dream chart because it always lifts my spirits." He concluded.

## Avoiding negative people

"Negative people always have a negative impact on the people around them because they constantly push ideas and people down. They should not get even a second of your time because all they do is drain your energy by creating unnecessary stress. If you spend time with a negative person, you will also become negative and good people will start to avoid you. Stay away from people who like gossiping, who play victim, people who manipulate others, people who judge you, people who never manage their emotions and arrogant people. A negative attitude is as infectious as any airborne disease. Those who have it can knowingly or unknowingly spread it to others. Avoid such people or you will soon be like them. He educated.

## Exercising regularly

"Exercise is very important for our health, to keep us fit and free from diseases. That is why we have a gym at home. Exercise also boosts our moods. You can walk, run or swim." Mr. Client explained.

## Getting a mentor

"A mentor is someone who has already achieved what you also want to achieve. You can learn all the skills and knowledge about a topic from a mentor. We should always find mentors in whatever we are doing. Even at school, we have mentors. This saves us from making many mistakes because the mentors always show us a clear path to follow." He said.

## Networking regularly

"Networking is important because it is a way to build long-term relationships and a good reputation over time. It involves meeting and getting to know people who can assist you and potentially help you. Your network includes everyone from friends and family to school and work colleagues and members of the communities to which we belong." He said.

## Continuous learning

"Continuous learning is about getting new skills every day." He began. "It is about updating the skills we have already acquired. It enables us to gain new skills, knowledge and information on an ongoing basis. Things change every day, so we have to be able to adapt to change. And the best way is by continuous learning. And learning never stops. Continuous learning is one of the most important habits in life." You must educate yourself all the time so that you remain relevant in a fast-changing world. He added.

I was learning so much about habits from this family than I had learnt my entire life. For me, what really started to stand out is that teaching was being done at the family level. These children were being schooled on how to be street smart and now to be relevant in life. School had its place in teaching them about Biology and Mathematics, but I saw that Mr. Client had converted the dinner table into a classroom of life. His children had a good start learning about money and success at an early age.

The children were learning and practicing these habits. It was a way of life for them. It wasn't like a requirement of sorts, just a way of life. It reminded me of the saying that if you teach children the way to go when they grow up, they will never depart from it. It is in seminars and conferences that we are normally taught the things that Mr. Client and Rose were teaching their children. I reflected on how I had grown up. None of this happened. My parents were hell-bent on disciplining us. It seemed as if all that they wanted of us is to be obedient. Somehow, they thought that obedience and passing our examinations in school will give us a brighter future than theirs – a good and noble intention. Even though these two things were important, they were just but a fraction of how the world works. Wealth and success are not built through being obedient, well-mannered and passing examinations. They are built through deliberate habits. There is a code of sorts that unlocks the treasure trove of wealth and that code's nervous system is habits.

I felt so humbled in the presence of Mr. Client and I knew that most definitely, I would borrow his way of life at home and use it in mine. My children will not be left to figure out how life works on their own. They will learn it from the dinner table. I thought that if I was exposed to this kind of information all my life as a child, I would probably have only myself to blame for not being successful. How blessed were these children in learning these things early in their lives? At times, people are poor because they were raised in a poor environment, but Mr. Client was raised in a poor environment and still made it rich. I perceived that his children have an abundance of options to pursue just about anything that they were passionate about in life for their parents would support them.

However, their parents were not taking their wealth for granted. They would rather see their children wealthy in knowledge, spirit and psyche than depend on material wealth that they didn't know how it was attained. I remembered how basketball legend Shaquille O'Neal answered a question about his family's wealth—talking about his children. He said in essence, *"I tell my children that we are not rich. I am rich. Not them. It is me who made the wealth and they will have to learn to make it themselves, then they can be rich.*" This is exactly what Mr. Client was doing with his children—teaching them how to be wealthy.

We ended the dinner and Mr. Client ushered me into his home library. It was a large room next to the living room. It had large windows and the inside had shelves lined with books on various subjects. It also had a sitting area with study tables. I couldn't help but ask how they were able to build so much success, both outside in business and at home with the family.

Then he told me that success is a 24-hour job, not a destination as most people think. He said success is something you work on for the rest of your life, and if you are not committed to it, don't even start on it.

"I don't advise you to get into something to which you aren't going to be committed for life. You must work hard and work smart." Don't listen to people who say you should only work smart - you need to put in time and effort until you have your desired results. He said.

By the end of the dinner, I had decided what I wanted most in my life: financial freedom, living a balanced happy and fulfilled life - financial freedom was going to be a part of this goal and not an end in itself.

We reviewed the lessons we had had since Monday – starting with a WHY, setting goals, paying yourself first, investing like the rich, creating multiple streams of income,

 *"it's not just a book… it's medicine."*

protecting your wealth, guarding and nourishing your thoughts, the enemies of success and the golden habits of success.

"Well, my friend, today is your graduation day," Mr. Client caught me off-guard.

"You mean that's it? I am through with the University of Wealth?" I quipped.

He chuckled.

"Tell me about your graduation from Law School." He asked.

"Well, there was a lot of fanfare at home and in the community. We had a great party, took photos and had speeches." I answered.

"You answer like my great German friend, straight forward, no details, no beating about the bush." He chuckled.

"That was just about it anyway."

"And then what happened?"

"I had to start looking for a job as a lawyer."

"So, what were you people celebrating at the party?"

"Well, successful attainment of a Law Degree, I suppose."

"Shall we celebrate the completion of your certificate in the University of Wealth?" He played along with my attempt at humor.

"It honestly feels weird to celebrate when I have nothing to show for it."

"I saw a meme the other day saying that just like women have inner beauty, men have inner money. Even though you don't see it, it's there." He smiled.

I roared in laughter.

"So, you are saying I have inner money?"

"I don't know. Do you?"

This was a serious question. Looking back at how I had started to dismantle my lifestyle and made some plans and commitments, looking at my resolve and some of the assignments that I would undertake to revolutionize my life that very week, I was confident of my answer to Mr. Client.

"I do have a lot of inner money; it's just waiting to manifest itself in the physical realm. I have to change myself, work hard and implement the lessons I have learned from you." I said while laughing but I was serious.

"Tell me about your inner money."

"If you take a look at how my mind has taken a beating by the concepts that you have been teaching me, if you look at what I have planned to do and the changes that I have instituted already, I do think I am on the path for success and financial freedom. Does that count for inner money?" I asked.

 *"it's not just a book… it's medicine."*

"Someone said that success is not a result of money, but money is a result of success. In other words, you form a success attitude and psyche—the so-called inner money, and the money becomes the byproduct."

"I hear you. So, am I really graduating today?"

"Well technically, yes. However, in the real sense, there can never be graduation from this. Our lessons end today and I am sure you have your work cut out for you. The ball is in your court. Again, technically, if you were to graduate, it will be when you have your first million dollars" he said with a serious tone.

Once your verifiable net worth hits one million United States Dollars, I will organize a graduation party for you and invite other self-made millionaires to share their success voyages with you. He promised.

"You think I have what it takes to make a million dollars?" I asked.

"It's long overdue, but I won't put pressure on you. It depends on how hungry you are for it." Mr. Client said.

I nodded somberly knowing full well that not only did I have the information to act upon, but I also had an accountability partner in Mr. Client. The goal was firmly engraved in my mind—to make a million dollars using the strategies already provided.

I left their home with a billionaire's mindset and a plan on how to earn my first million dollars.

The assignment was tough, but my resolve was even tougher. There were very many setbacks on the road, but I kept my eyes on the prize. Some things were obvious to do and implement but I found that mastering different financial streams was the game changer for me. My colleagues started noticing a big difference in my life and attitude and they made comments about it. Some of them complained that I was no longer going out with them for drinks and parties but in actuality, I had culled them from off my life due to their negative influence on my success journey. Soon enough, I was championing two ideas that I knew would solve problems for people in my community and could even be scaled to the whole country and other parts of the world. The progress was slow and at times it felt like the business idea would never see the light of the day. There was so much to learn from the process. I kept my day job but at the corner of my eye, I knew that I was on the way out. I needed to grow bigger and fly alone like an eagle if I was ever to attain the million-dollar mark.

One of the greatest schoolings I had learnt from Mr. Client and his family was that as a man shapes a beautiful plate from a pile of dirty clay so does he craft his own destiny… he must not blame anyone for how the plate turns out, he alone is responsible for the results of his life. He must eat from his plate.

If you are serious about financial freedom and success, if you are tired of the life, you are living and want to see a difference; I implore you to do the same. List down five

 *"it's not just a book… it's medicine."*

reasons why you deserve to be successful. Don't wait. Do that right now before you read the next sentence. Do it now and not tomorrow - the trick lies in taking action not the endless accumulation of knowledge. These reasons will be your source of strength when the rough times come – and for sure they will come.

You will not be able to implement everything at once. You don't have to.

This book is not just a read through guide, it is a worksheet to be implemented. Work through chapter one right now, then start working on the next chapter as you implement. Take action. You will get much better results. I did so and it changed my life.

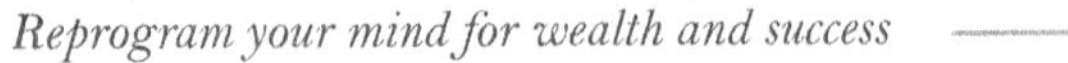

www.ingramcontent.com/pod-product-compliance
Lightning Source LLC
Chambersburg PA
CBHW051822150726
47998CB00001B/250